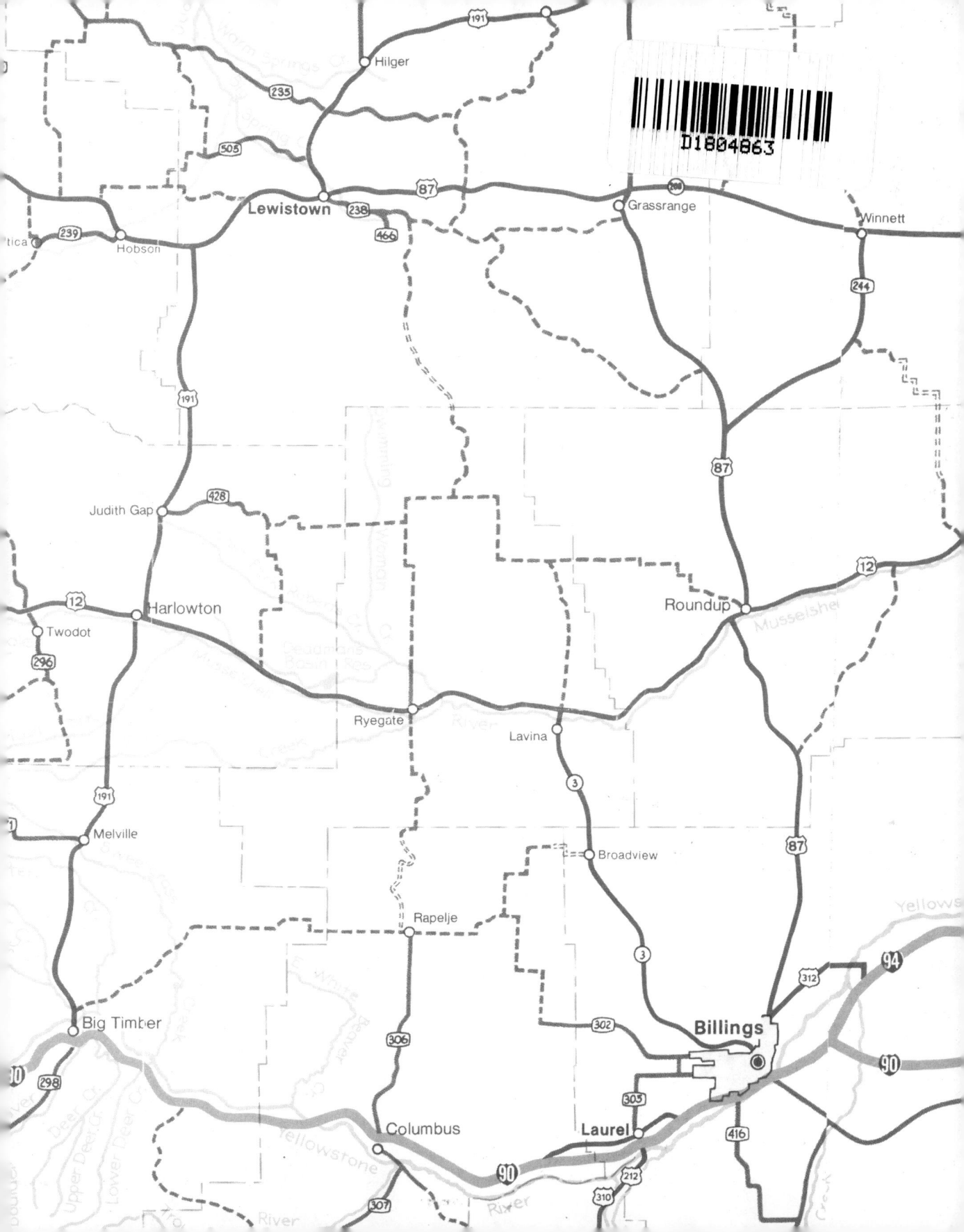

Mist on the River:

Remembrances of Dan Bailey

By Charles F. Waterman

Mist on the River:

Remembrances of Dan Bailey

By Charles F. Waterman

Tribute by Lee Wulff

Illustrated and designed by Victoria Kuser

YELLOWSTONE PRESS ● Livingston, Montana

Copyright ©1986 by Yellowstone Press

ALL RIGHTS RESERVED. No part of this book may be used or reproduced in any manner whatsoever without prior permission from the publisher except in the case of brief quotations embodied in critical reviews and articles. All inquiries should be addressed to Yellowstone Press, PO Box 1019, Livingston, MT 59047

Produced by
Yellowstone Press
PO Box 1019
Livingston, MT 59047

Published and distributed by
Yellowstone Press
PO Box 1019
Livingston, MT 59047

PRINTED IN THE UNITED STATES OF AMERICA

ISBN 0-9617253-0-3

All photographs are by the author except those which are credited on the page they appear.

CONTENTS

DAN BAILEY, A TRIBUTE ix

INTRODUCTION xiii

I

ONE	*Just the Facts*	1
TWO	*Trout Advocate*	17
THREE	*Where the Flies Are Made*	23
FOUR	*Tackle Matters*	35
FIVE	*The Tank Fish*	39
SIX	*Hunting Trips*	43
SEVEN	*Away From Home*	51
EIGHT	*The Little Creeks*	55
NINE	*The Hunting Lodge*	59
TEN	*Rod, Reel and Fly*	65

II DAN BAILEY'S WATER 77

ONE	*The Yellowstone*	79
TWO	*Spring Creeks*	93
THREE	*Sweetgrass*	103
FOUR	*Rock Creek*	107
FIVE	*Madison River*	111
SIX	*The Firehole*	119
SEVEN	*Middle Creek*	125
EIGHT	*Sheep Creek*	129
NINE	*The Missouri*	133
TEN	*The Gallatin*	139
ELEVEN	*The Jefferson*	145
TWELVE	*Slough Creek*	149
THIRTEEN	*Boulder River*	153
FOURTEEN	*Beaverhead River*	157
FIFTEEN	*Big Hole River*	161
SIXTEEN	*Smith River*	165
SEVENTEEN	*Bighorn River*	169
EIGHTEEN	*The Henry's Fork*	173
NINETEEN	*Some Park Waters*	177
TWENTY	*The Shields River*	185
TWENTY ONE	*Another Bailey*	189
	Epilogue	193

DAN BAILEY, A tribute

Dan Bailey was a good man. He was good at fishing and fly tying and the things he loved to do. He was a good friend, honorable, a thorough gentleman and a wonderful companion. I respected and admired him as much as any man I have known.

We fished the Catskill streams and New York's Ausable in the late twenties and early thirties together. We were not a part of the well known group that alternated their fishing of the Beaverkill with frequent social drinks at the Antrim Lodge. We camped out and we fished from dawn till dark. There was so much to learn and so much to enjoy, our weekends were too short not to spend all our available time on the streams.

Throughout the years Dan gave me a host of treasured memories. He showed me Armstrong's Creek in Montana when it still ran freely into the Yellowstone and the big fish from that river came up into its clear, cool waters to supplement its great native stock when the big river grew overly warm. Together we fished the streams of the Yellowstone area with the same fervor we'd fished the Ausable and the Saranac. Dan stayed in the West and I concentrated on Atlantic Salmon in Eastern Canada but whenever I went west Dan was always there with the same warmth of humor and friendship.

I can remember Dan's low chuckle and excitement when we were walking along 9th Street in the Greenwich Village section of New York where we both lived and looked up to see, in a second story window a sign that read, "O.B. Fish/Feathers." We climbed the stairs to find a short, round Englishman who imported from Asia and India the most exciting assortment of feathers we'd ever seen.

I will be forever indebted to Dan for his companionship and inspiration. Indebted, too, because it was Dan who insisted on the giving of my name to the Wulff Series and gave me stature I might never have had otherwise. We were fishing together on the Esopus in the spring of 1930 when I was trying out some new flies I'd designed in revolt to the then available Catskill patterns. The new flies had bucktail wings and tails for better flotation. They had heavier bodies that offered a trout a better reward for his rise. They were durable. I'd made them to imitate the coffin mayfly and the big gray drakes that hatched in the Ausable in September and to replace the spin-prone, ultra-fragile Fanwing Coachman. I had planned to call them the Coffin May, the Ausable Gray and the Bucktail Coachman. It was Dan who insisted that I call them Wulffs and he started tying them under that name. It was Dan who sat with me to work out the other patterns of the series, the Grizzly, the Black, The Blonde and the rest to give a greater range to this new category of flies that floated on animal hair. When Dan moved west he took the Catskill tradition of fly tying as well as the new patterns that developed there to the western streams and changed the trout fishing world out there.

Dan not only loved fishing but he loved fishermen. He was never too busy to advise on where to fish and what techniques to use. He was most generous of his secrets and his secret spots were then secret no more. He was a man to love and I miss him.

Mist on the River:
Remembrances of Dan Bailey

Dan Bailey

Introduction

This is about Dan Bailey, his fishing, the places he fished and some of the people who played parts in his life. He said there was nothing unusual about his life except that people had been so good to him. He said he was very lucky.

It is not stylish to say that a successful man is lucky — whether he becomes rich or famous or simply lives a happy life, but there was some luck in Dan Bailey's life — as he insisted there was.

Begin with his real name — Dan Bailey — which sounds good in a fishing story, somehow fits well in the fishing tackle business, and is as good or better than most of the fictitious names attached to outdoor products. Begin with the timing with which he cut his academic ties in the East and went to Montana just as Western trout fishing was opening up. Begin with his choice of what he thought would be the best trout fishing place in the world. There was some luck there all right. And maybe Dan Bailey's attitude toward life and the outdoors in itself was lucky.

Dan always said he never understood why but he became an institution that used to cut through commercialism. Many years ago I found that an editor who would delete other references to specific tackle companies would accept Dan Bailey's name happily, actually feeling that it added prestige to an article. It was good strategy to insert Dan Bailey's opinion of something.

The Bailey business and reputation were built largely through correspondence and if Dan received an inquiry about fishing in the Montana area he simply sat down and answered it personally with his pipe and portable typewriter. Through the years this became a tremendous volume of correspondence and he evidently enjoyed the whole thing. As time went on, fishing name droppers spoke of Dan as a close friend, even though they had never seen him.

He watched the trout scene change and although he was quite aware of the nuances of scientific angling, he laughed gently at it.

"They come through the door talking Latin now," he said a few years ago. And now and then, although no one would suspect soft-spoken Dan of sarcasm, he would kid an over-scientific fisherman just a little — softly and only for his private amusement.

Dan didn't really look like Dan Bailey at first glance. He was a rather small man, weighing around 145 pounds, and I guess most of the correspondents who saw him for the first time had a different mental picture of him. In the routine misjudgement of small men, hardly anyone noticed that he was an athlete. Fact is, he had been a gymnast in his youth and he was muscular. He had the sloping shoulders that often go with compact men. I once described him as having the "boxer's slightly rounded shoulders" and it was the only time Dan ever took exception to anything I wrote.

"What you said about me was very flattering in other respects," Dan said firmly, "but I do not have round shoulders."

I didn't argue but I think you know what I mean. The "round" business comes from what have been described as "hitting muscles" about the shoulder blades.

Anyway, Bailey was, as hunters and hikers often say, "tough in the mountains." He was an exceptional wader with the logical mixture of daring and perception. He was smaller than most of the good waders, "good" meaning the ability to stay dry and balanced in fast, deep water over slippery bottom. So we tell our first Dan Bailey story and must watch it or we'll end up with a book full of them, which isn't the idea.

It was early fall, the time when big brown trout acquire their mating colors and are likely to take big streamers or giant nymphs. Three of us were drifting the Yellowstone and Dan was rowing the aluminum johnboat between fishing spots. The trip was for the special entertainment of a visitor from the East, a big, powerful guy who liked to double haul with a big rod and watch a heavy shooting head cross the river. He didn't have a spare line with him.

It could have happened to anybody, I guess. The big guy cast across a fast stretch studded with boulders and he hung up across one of them. You could see part of the dark green shooting head draped just above the water line. And the water sloped visibly, too fast to row against. The boat was beached below the hangup.

"I guess I'm out of business," the Easterner said as he pulled so hard his monofilament running line broke.

"Oh, I think I can get it for you," Dan said. The guest laughed. Dan walked upstream along the rocky bank. The guest was quiet.

Dan simply walked out into the river and came dancing down toward the boulder and the line. The heavy water was near his wader tops and there was no stopping once the trip began. Dan pirouetted along, gracefully plucked the lost line from the boulder and went on down below us, working gradually toward shore and looking for a landing spot. He then walked back up the shoreline to hand the line to its owner. He was 60 years old and completely dry but his pipe had gone out.

There was one strange loyalty in Dan that seemed to go beyond the call of duty. He felt as someone who made his living from fly fishermen he should do his own fishing at the customer's level. Sound funny? It worked like this:

It's true that, occasionally, Dan would make exotic fishing trips. Occasionally, he would be the guest of someone with exclusive "private" water. But he said:

"If I'm going to talk about fishing to tourist fishermen I should fish where they fish. If property is closed to most of the public, I don't think I should spend much of my time there."

This philosophy seemed a little strange to Dan himself and he would chuckle apologetically when he explained it, but he stuck by it most of the time.

Dan Bailey with a big brown trout in
New Zealand.

ONE

Just the Facts

When he was driving along the Mexican coast on the Baja Peninsula in recent years, Dan Bailey was likely to simply pull off the road with his car and trailer, walk over to the surf and start fly casting. It didn't matter whether it was known as a fishing spot or not.

It was the same in Montana, where Dan was likely to catch trout in a creek he didn't know the name of — if it had a name — and if he didn't catch trout there he would begin a personal investigation to find why not. He was an angling explorer, something often overlooked by his friends. When he settled firmly in Montana he did it because he thought he had found the country's best trout fishing. Like others who have followed trout to the beautiful parts of the world, Bailey was outspoken in his choice.

"This is a big country," he wrote. "The trout streams are big, the trout are big and there is plenty of elbow room. We consider our Yellowstone River crowded when there is more than one angler per mile of water............It is a depressing thought that a lifetime is not long enough to fish all of the good spots out here."

That appeared in 1952 in the Fishing & Hunting News, published in Portland, Oregon and it is about as near as he ever came to flamboyant language. Most of his writing was in letters to those who inquired about fishing, although after his death there was a brief outline among his papers, evidently the beginnings of a book that was never written. He did no personal promotion on his own, but Bailey and his way of life were irresistible to professional writers, photographers and film makers, something that he said he never understood.

"I don't know why all of these people are so good to us," he once said as if he were speaking to himself. He'd been talking about interviews and fishing trips scheduled for several outdoor writers and photographers. Then, as usual, he repeated his business philosophy.

"I didn't intend for the business to get this big," he said, almost regretfully. "I just wanted to go fishing."

But he was a good businessman in the final analysis and he used opportunities for business promotion, even when he did not instigate them himself.

Dan Bailey was born in 1904 and grew up on a farm near Russelville in southwestern Kentucky. Writers have been tempted to make him into a Huck Finn but it doesn't quite fit. The evolution from barefoot worm fisherman for farm pond crappies to a consummate fly caster for difficult trout started pretty early.

At that time the fly rod for bass was really more popular than it was later on. Baitcasting tackle of the twenties was rather awkward and the heavy-spooled reels of that time were not well-adapted to light lures. Dan started fishing for smallmouth bass with flies he tied himself, a sport considered quite similar to trout fishing. Spinning tackle for America was 30 years away and flies were the expert's method.

Bailey attended the Citadel, where he graduated in 1926. That background would have assured him of an officer's commission during World War II and was the basis for an important decision he made when the war started, but from the Citadel he went to the University of Kentucky and earned a master's degree in physics.

Trout fishing came in when he taught for a year at Jefferson City Junior College in Missouri and he did it at Bennett Springs in the Ozarks. At that time Missouri rivers were more noted for smallmouth bass drift fishing but there were several with trout. Bennett Springs and Roaring River State Parks were carefully managed for trout fishing.

From Missouri, Bailey went to teach at Lehigh University in Pennsylvania and there were the trout again, especially trout in famous and difficult streams. Technical fishing. By 1930 he was in New York to teach at Brooklyn Polytechnic Institute and began work on a Ph.D. in physics at New York University. Now farther away from the trout, he became closer to the inner circle of trout fishing and fell in more and more with those who shared his passion and who were to be well known in the field.

Lee Wulff, a commercial artist at the time, joined Bailey to conduct a fly-tying school. Apparently their names were not much attraction then and they drew only one student, a corporate lawyer named John J. McCloy, later to be a presidential advisor. The fly-tying school was attended by another, however, John McDonald, writer for Fortune Magazine and later a Fortune editor. McDonald had become a close friend of Bailey (a lifetime association) and was a sort of polite shill for the school — but evidently it was no great success anyway. It was located behind Lee Chumley's Restaurant in Greenwich Village.

By then Bailey was an angling sophisticate and fished as many as possible of the trout streams within reach, such as the Beaverkill, Neversink and Willowmoc of lower New York. There were many others.

There was angling tradition in the Catskills and Adirondacks in those times of the Great Depression and New Yorkers, as a group, were the most prominent of American trout fishermen. Even the steelhead followers of the West Coast were not so well known. The "father of dry fly fishing in America," Theodore Gordon, had practiced his art in the Catskills and, after all, it hadn't been so long since he had done so.

McDonald, a writing scholar, did not separate his avocation from his profession. His works on fly fishing included thoughtful studies on the history of angling and he was intrigued by the life of Theodore Gordon. McDonald, who was later to be a vital part of Bailey's success, did more than anyone else to bring posthumous recognition to Gordon. This is important because it is more of the atmosphere that Bailey lived in. Fly fishermen tend to read and write more than other fishermen and the shelves of angling literature prove it.

In some six years in New York, Bailey became acquainted with many of the great fly tiers and authorities on the subject, most of whom were centered in the East and who sought each other out. There were the Harry Darbees, the Walt Dettes, Reuben Cross and Preston Jennings. Years later, when Paul Young, the rod maker, brought a "bundle" of rods to Montana, Dan caught a 4-pounder with one of the lighter ones Young asked him to test. In time, Jim Deren of New York's famous Angler's Roost fished with Dan in Montana as did many of the others. It was to become a sort of Mecca for Eastern trout seekers.

Ed Zern, famous outdoor writer and humorist, told of "heading for Montana from New York and driving straight through, changing off and stopping only for gas and food." Years later, Joe Brooks was to say, "Montana is just one day farther than the rest of the Western trout fishing. It's not crowded."

Bailey continually sought new and better fishing places, sometimes gleefully discovering the secret spots of angling authors. He kept the secrets well but in later years gloated over his findings.

"I finally figured out where Ray Bergman was catching trout near New York," he said. And much later he said he had figured where Ted Trueblood was catching steelhead. Trueblood undoubtedly acknowledged it when he and Dan became frequent fishing companions later on.

During the New York years Dan shared a Catskill cabin with Ivan Bloch, son of the composer Ernest Bloch. That was on Liebhardt Creek and that is where the "Wallfish," a long-time trademark of Bailey's Fly Shop, got its start, but it was no promotion to begin with.

John McDonald, who was there at its beginning, explains the origin of the Wall Of Fame. He first met Dan in 1935 and learned his basic fly fishing from him. Then in 1936 he and Dan used the Catskill cabin that Dan and Bloch had shared in the 1935 season. When he arrived there McDonald saw the outline of a 15-inch brown trout traced on one of the interior walls. It was inscribed "July 14, 1935/by Dan."

They decided that no trout would be outlined there unless it was larger than the last, and when McDonald posted the next outline it was after the Baileys had gone West. In seven years McDonald outlined four fish, the largest of which was 18 inches. He and his wife Dorothy continued to use the Liebhardt cabin until World War II. McDonald, in a letter to Rod & Reel after

The Liebhardt cottage of the Thirties - once known as "The Tenement."

Dan and Helen Bailey on the porch of their Eastern fishing cabin in the Thirties.

Dan's death, explained that Liebhardt Creek was a tributary of the Rondout River and that all of the first wall fish came from the creek. He explained that the larger fish that came up from the river could not be handled in the creek's cramped quarters.

The old cabin, McDonald explained, was beginning to disintegrate when he abandoned it. It had two floors and had housed two lumbermen's families before 1900 so the old residents had called it "The Tenement." McDonald cut out the section of wall that bore the "wall fish." They were the beginning of a much better know series of outlines that was to appear in the Montana shop.

Dan was married to Helen Hesslein in 1936. At the time, Helen was living in Greenwich Village and working as a public health nurse. She and John McDonald's new wife Dorothy were long-time friends.

Dan taught Helen to fish with flies and many years later there were reports that she was an exceptionally talented angler but it wasn't so. Although she loved the outdoors and spent many nights in tents and trailers in all sorts of weather, Helen's interest was more in the things that went with fishing than in the fishing itself. She insisted that she was clumsy with a rod and continually laughed at the problems she had in fly casting. She also insisted none of her trips was complete until she had fallen in at least once. She was to catch some exceptional fish in many places, but when the Bailey's were on a stream she spent more time reading than casting. She became a fine camp cook.

From the first the Bailey's had planned a honeymoon trip to Montana and their wedding presents were assorted items of camping equipment. Dan had read a great deal about the area but at that time few trout fishermen would go from East or West Coast to an area largely undeveloped as tourist country except for Yellowstone National Park. Dan credited a descriptive article in the Billings Gazette as the final inducement.

Helen's introduction to Montana trout fishing was abrupt. Dan began exploring immediately and headed up an old mining road near Cooke City. The road was bad and the mountain was

high. The car suffered altitude sickness, a common ailment of autos in those days, and stopped, so they camped where the car quit. Helen, also a victim of the altitude, felt very strange and said she suspected she was losing her mind.

But most of the trip was spent on the Madison and Gallatin Rivers and Dan was completely captured by the Big Sky Country and its trout. They were back in Montana the next year too and Helen returned early to New York to continue her nursing work while Dan explored more trout streams.

Then Dan, whose specialty was atomic physics, decided he'd rather try to make a living tying flies and abandoned his efforts toward a Ph.D., although he hadn't far to go. He said later that atomic physics was then a field whose time had not really come anyway, and added that he was "no Einstein." If he ever regretted his choice he never admitted it. He was willing to work however hard and long was necessary to get all of the fishing he wanted but he was going to do it in what he considered the best trout country in America. For Helen, it would be a complete uprooting — a separation from her beloved New York and a voyage into uncertainty. Their friends in New York considered Montana a sort of frontier and the Baileys had no true contact there. They didn't know where they would settle but Dan thought it would be in the Bozeman-Livingston vicinity.

Fate interfered on what is known as Bozeman Hill, which is topped by Bozeman Pass, separating Bozeman from Livingston. While Helen was driving and they were climbing up the Livingston side, they ran off the road, damaging an axle. Since it was easier to go down than up, they limped back to Livingston. The two towns are about 26 miles apart and at that time the Livingston population was about 7,000.

Dan said later that if they had gotten a few miles further before the accident they would have coasted into Bozeman instead and that's where he would have gone into business. He said also that he would have been less successful in Bozeman. Livingston grew only slightly in the ensuing years while Bozeman became much larger. Since he had less local trade in Livingston he found it necessary to go into wholesale and mailorder business. In Bozeman, he felt, he would have relied too much on local customers.

In Livingston they opened a shop at the old Albermarle Hotel with living quarters in back for $25 a month. Dan already had a modest business in mailorder flies and he went to work, got credit from some tackle companies and was in business. As early as 1936 he had advertised his flies in Outdoor Life, giving a winter address in New York and a summer address as "General Delivery, Ennis, Montana." Ennis is located on the Madison.

An early Bailey camp in Montana. Left to right: Mrs. Preston Jennings, Ken Reid (Chicago writer), Helen Bailey, Preston Jennings, Dan Bailey.

They opened a shooting gallery in the first Bailey store, complete with moving targets and twenty-two rifles and pistols. No partition between the tackle and the shooting. Red Monical, who began tying flies at that time, said the noise didn't bother the fly tackle customers much because most of the shooting was in the evening. But Red and Jimmy Lees, another young tier, got in some daytime practice when Dan was gone. Red, 14 years old at the time, said that they'd temporarily abandon their work and go over to the gallery to "shoot some of Dan's ammunition." Had Red known he would later be a partner in the store he might have been more jealous of the resources.

There was a minor inconvenience concerning the shooting gallery. The Baileys' sleeping quarters were immediately behind the backstop and Helen reported the attendant noise was disturbing, whether she was attempting to sleep or read in bed. She reported quantities of lead fragments continually showered on her cot. It was not a matter of insufficient backstop but the 22 bullets apparently spattered and powdered and the particles sifted through.

Besides the shooting gallery of the Thirties, there was another project to supplement the fly and tackle sales — commercial whitefishing on the Yellowstone. The Baileys became whitefish dealers and handled shipments through their store.

Red Monical and Gilbert Meloche, another Bailey employee, did considerable commercial whitefishing and their methods bear recording. They used cane poles and stood on the river bank with a tub between them. The short lines were fastened to small flies with the barbs bent down and maggots were added for bait.

"The fly," Red said, "was an attractor."

Hooked whitefish were flopped neatly into the tub in a sort of miniature of offshore tuna operations. Experience helped for concentrations of whitefish must be discoverd before operations began.

The whitefish business was concluded because of legal problems. While Dan and Helen were away an employee who was supposed to handle the whitefish went to jail for non-support, leaving a quantity of unrefrigerated whitefish in the store. Helen reported that the resultant odor was both penetrating and persistent.

But the Baileys learned a great deal about whitefish and "grub flies" were good sellers, whether used with natural bait or not. The status of the Rocky Mountain whitefish, which reaches considerable size in Montana streams, has been rather vague. Some ardent trout fishermen who despise their sucker-mouthed appearance, and who expect to release their fish anyway, will admit they often can't tell whether they have a trout or a whitefish until it is ready to net. One is a cause for rejoicing and

Gilbert Meloche with the first big trout to make the Montana Hall of Fame.

the other a disappointment. But the whitefish, which don't jump when hooked unless given a bit of help from the rod, are said by most anglers to fight harder than grayling of the same size.

The imitation grub flies were hardly aesthetic designs and Red said their construction was relegated to beginning fly tiers or those who showed little aptitude for more artistic production.

Meloche, who cooperated with Red on whitefish projects, was, nevertheless, highly critical of the youthful tier's flies. He was inclined to pull them apart in enthusiastic testing.

"I learned to tie the tightest damned squirrel hair flies in the country," Red said. "Meloche would jerk them apart if they weren't."

Red, who had started fly tying with a simple kit before becoming a professional, was helped by Jimmy Lees and Dan. Something that happened at about that time may have influenced Dan toward women tiers, Red said. It seems that Jimmy suddenly began to turn in better flies than ever before and while admiring the improved quality Dan learned that Jimmy's mother was doing a considerable share of the work.

Meloche, an ardent trout angler, is recognized as the first to make the Wall Of Fame in the Montana store. The requirement was and is that a fish must weigh four pounds. Later, that limit was applied to stream fish only while it took a 10-pounder to "make the wall" from a lake.

The Meloche fly, still in the catalog, is very light in color and was introduced when Meloche came in from Armstrong Spring Creek, where he had encountered a profuse hatch. He had captured one of the flies and had it in his hat for copying. With the imitation he returned to the creek and caught the first Montana Wall Fish. At that time the spring creeks were something of a secret as they would have been vulnerable to overfishing and Meloche's catch was credited to the Yellowstone.

Much of the early fly tying was impromptu and one of the first of the tiers was Frances DePuy (later Mrs. William Platania), who was in the shop for years. At one time it was common for a fisherman to simply walk into the store, ask her what the fish were taking, and get what was needed, even if he waited for it — true custom tying.

Early bookkeeping methods were rather simple. Dan simply wrote all of his checks, personal or otherwise, from a single account, and since the records were skimpy he found himself in a jam when one employee held her checks for years without cashing them. Upon demand for the money, Dan found the account was a little short.

Although Helen helped out in the store at one time, she spent considerable periods working in New York during the early years, ever doubtful that the Montana project would succeed. She finally "moved completely" to Montana and began work as a school nurse there. At times during the early years, Dan served as a substitue teacher in Livingston.

World War II was a special crisis to the Baileys. Dan could have had a captaincy if he had gone into armed service but Helen, having suffered the agony of one separation from New York, refused to endure it again. She said that if Dan went into military service and she were forced to return to New York she had no intentions of going back to Montana. Then the government expressed doubt that the maufacture of fishing flies was essential to the war effort. Dan went to work as a railway brakeman but continued to tie flies. The store was "in a way" open during the war.

Red Monical went to war and when he brought his two Purple Hearts back from the South Pacific he took up where he had left off. Both he and Dan were tying flies along with others but Red had ambition of being a part owner in the store and had saved for it. He bought in as a junior partner, continuing a low-key presence — so low-key that few have realized he is a member of the firm. He felt that Dan, already well-known to the world's famous fishermen, would always be the "front man," which he was. So unassuming was Red's wartime departure and return that one former employee inquired as to "how Red Monical stayed out of the army."

His name is not prominent in trout fishing literature but Red's line has reached across the river for many outdoor photographers and many a big trout in promotional photos has come to Red's flies. When the big streamers came to the rivers, Red became one of the "long casters" for fall browns.

Real development of the Bailey business began in the Fifties. The store was moved to its more recent location on Park Street, nearly all of the equipment carried by hand, and some tears were shed by those who had seen the beginnings.

It is obvious now why Dan Bailey was so "lucky." He was in business at the right time in the right place and had come from the right place to get there. He was a highly literate man who generally had an "upstairs book" and a "downstairs book" being read at the same time. he was already known to a very large share of the trout fishing intelligencia of the East, and that was where the serious trout fishermen were centered.

No matter how many cows Dan Bailey ran on his ranch or how far he wandered into the Montana back country he still retained and would always retain ties to the East, ties strengthened by Helen's New York roots. A traveling angler from far away cities had a readymade contact in Livingston. Bailey automatically knew the visitor's fishing problems for he had encountered them himself at an earlier time.

As Dan became still better known, an invitation to the Bailey ranch or later to their Livingston homes became prized among the visitors. Helen loved to cook and loved to entertain informally and her meals were treasured although she used to say, "I don't have a very exclusive taste. I tend to just order eggs in a restaurant."

The invitations were almost invariably extended for "after fishing," meaning a late evening dinner during the long summer days. Dan didn't always know who was coming to dinner but Helen made constant effort at learning who was "in town" and on the streams. And when Dan could get away from the store in those days he very frequently took a visiting angler with him. He might go upstream while the guest went down but there is no telling how many people have "gone fishing with Dan Bailey."

Then there were the non-fishing wives, more plentiful than most articles about fishing would indicate. The wives came to Livingston, probably visited Yellowstone Park and were just beginning to run out of things to do when they received gracious invitations for dinner "after fishing." Then, if they had not already known, they found that they were to be entertained by a hostess who had been reared in New York, was transplanted to Montana and who spoke their language, even after some twenty years on the frontier. And they learned from their husbands that Dan Bailey was famous.

Then there were the fishing writers. The Bailey business was just novel enough that editors were willing to run stories about the man who sold the flies as well as about the trout that took them. And the Bailey story fitted into publications besides the hook and bullet magazines. The truly literary articles by John McDonald crossed into a more general field. Then there were the television people.

Montana had become conscious of tourism and began to promote fishing and hunting so outdoor writers were especially welcome. The Montana Chamber of Commerce hosted dozens of them and Bill Browning headed that program, first as executive secretary of the Chamber and then as outdoor host.

Joe Brooks, who began regular trips to Montana in the Fifties, became a constant asset to Bailey's. He was famous as an angler and fishing writer and he and his wife Mary made their summer headquarters at Livingston, living at first in a cabin at the Edwin Nelson ranch where Nelson's Spring Creek is located. On his last day of each season Brooks insisted upon going fishing with both Red and Dan. He was literally followed to Montana and to Bailey's by dozens of fly fishermen, many of whom became annual visitors. They bought summer homes and they headquartered at the Bailey store, which acquired a clublike atmosphere.

Dan Bailey was patiently helpful to the writers, some of whom produced sheaves of articles about the area. One of the most prolific, Erwin Bauer, made the photograph of the Royal Wulff fly and fisherman that has appeared on years of Bailey catalogs —almost as much a trademark as is the looped fly leader and attached fly which Dan adopted early in the game.

Dan's attitude was that all of these stories and films were good for business, promoted his beloved Montana and gave opportunity for conservation messages. As his face became familiar to environmentalists his advice was sought on ecological problems and his support was valuable in any such project.

Through the years Bailey acquired numerous nearby competitors in the tackle field and always insisted they were good for business. There were numerous attemps at buying all or part of the fly shop, some of them by large concerns. One business-suited group (looking a bit out of place at the fly counter) briskly

"The Montana Chamber of Commerce hosted dozens of them (outdoor writers) and Bill Browning headed that program."
(Bill Browning with a big brown trout on the Beaverhead.)

began confident negotiations, which ended up in the local coffee shop. They learned the fly business was as much Dan Bailey's life as his fishing was and he simply didn't want to sell. Money, it seemed, was not a factor in the decision.

"What would I do if I didn't have the store?" Dan asked. "I'll be here until they carry me out."

John Bailey came home from college and the army and moved into the business where he and his father worked together. Daughter Sue became a computer systems analyst. Things were going pretty well but Dan Bailey had a reservation.

"Too many people will come to Montana," he said, "and it's partly my fault."

Bill Browning Photo

Joe Brooks fishes for evening browns on the Musselshell, a prairie river.

TWO

Trout Advocate

Records show that most ardent conservationists are active for only short parts of their lives. Generally they come on the scene rapidly and fade the same way, either tired of an endless fight or feeling they have done their share and that it's time for new blood.

Dan Bailey had been a conservationist from his youth and remained active through his life. He was in the Izaac Walton League very early and Red Monical recalls that he insisted on paying for a membership for Red too. When Dan first went to Montana fish were a minor factor in land and water management but he neglected no opportunity to stand up for trout. Later, he was a leader in Trout Unlimited, but he was quick to join any organization he felt was a worthwhile movement for the ecology.

He worked for wilderness areas he could never enjoy first hand. Through all of his endless appearances at meetings and contributions to conservation organizations, Bailey's constant purpose was aid for the public in use of the outdoors. Even where it became obvious that a fishery could not be maintained for the general public, Bailey tended to give ground grudgingly. With public access to waters and forests as his contant objective, the European system of private ownership of fish and game offended him. He was an admirer of the New Zealand policy of free access to waters and to adjoining land although he realized that there must be restraint in heavily populated areas.

His outspoken stance in support of Wild and Scenic Rivers programs sometimes turned ranchers against him — usually, only temporarily.

"Sometimes, in trying to get everybody into fishing water I end

Joe Brooks, visiting author, takes a fine rainbow trout on Rock Creek near Missoula Montana.

Bill Browning Photo

up being locked out myself," he grumbled good-naturedly. But if his name and business earned him special treatment he was inclined to decline it.

From the first, the Yellowstone River got his protection, and needed it. The best-known of the Yellowstone issues has been the repeatedly proposed Allen Spur Dam, which would turn much of Paradise Valley, south of Livingston, into a lake, flooding ranchland and eliminating miles of river fishing. It was first proposed about 1902. Paradise Valley got its name, it is reported, when Texas cowmen sought it as a bad weather haven for herds on the move.

The Allen Spur Dam, its name coming from a railway designation, would span a canyon just south of Livingston and would back up water for more than 30 miles. Waters that flooded Paradise Valley would irrigate arid sections farther down and could provide power. Then came growth of the coal industry and proposals for Yellowstone water to carry coal to far away plants. Increased interest in the environment has held off the dam but as Dan Bailey said, the battle for free-flowing water is never ending and there will ever be new projects to harness it. One aid came from an unexpected source when it was revealed that seismic activity might endanger downstream populations. Yellowstone Park and the land about it shiver regularly with earthquakes, small and large.

In many ways the Yellowstone has improved as a blue ribbon trout river, partly through human intervention and partly through the continual repair work of nature. Dan Bailey surprised some old residents in recent years when he reported stream improvement while they bewailed what they considered a downhill trend.

When the Baileys camped near Cooke City half a century ago the river carried the refuse from mountainsides pierced by countless mines and prospecting holes. And Montana land carried its millions of sheep, the bands marked by the white dots of sheepherders' arks on a thousand slopes. The sheep industry, much smaller as the years went by, had been very hard on the land in many places.

Then there came the garbage discard of a populace that for a long while regarded a river as a public disposal plant. That, for the most part, was a cosmetic curse but it hurt the angler's "experience," a term scoffed at by residents who hadn't really looked that closely at their river. He was sensitive to an old car body used as a seawall and Dan Bailey was one of those rare individuals who picked up other people's trash at a river access point.

Now the river has improved in gradual ways that Bailey noted. At one time there were hardly any fly hatches above Yankee Jim

Canyon, the stretch of fast water below Gardiner, and that changed as the water ran cleaner. According to Bailey the cottus, bullhead or sculpin was a resident only of tributary streams at one time, coming into the main river as the water purified. The Muddler Minnow followed the bullhead into cleaner water.

Fly hatches have changed. It is said that the very largest of the stone flies — the "salmon fly"— may have been introduced by fishermen from the Madison. It is relatively new in the Yellowstone. To the frustration of entomologists who prefer more exact designations, observers say that one large "trout fly" (a slightly smaller stone fly) has disappeared.

It is easy to be carried away by the Yellowstone story because it is so long a stretch of free flowing river and because so many changes and battles have occurred in Dan Bailey's lifetime. At least the river exhibits some of the environmental efforts that have become stylish in recent years, and the situation is somewhat different from what it was in 1959 when Dan Bailey wrote the following for the Park County News:

"In spite of the high value of our recreation industry little is done to conserve it, to say nothing of improving it. At the same time, great effort is being expended to bring in new industries of questionable value and developments which might lead to new industry. Why should we not put more effort into saving and expanding the great recreation industry which we already have?"

Trout Unlimited fit Bailey's philosophy of trout and trout waters and he was at the organization of Montana's first chapter in West Yellowstone at Bud Lilly's. Others there included Lilly, Joe Halterman, Bud Morris, Merton Parks, John Peters and Pat Sample. Bailey served as a national director for some time. He was named to the Fishing Hall of Fame as the organization began.

Along with his legacy of personal effort in behalf of trout and the wild places, Bailey left a stack of membership cards. Among them were those from The Nature Conservancy, Izaac Walton League, Ducks Unlimited, Trout Unlimited, Montana Wildlife Federation, the Wilderness Society and the Sierra Club.

Through years of consistent personal policy and faithful attendance when conservation policies were made, Bailey was well-known in legislative circles. Jim Possewitz, veteran Fish and Game Commission conservation worker, found that when Dan Bailey was present legislators became available.

Ray Hurley, who had engaged in Trout Unlimited lobbying, said wonderingly: "With Posewitz I found that although people might be hard to run down at other times they seemed to come out of the woodwork with their hands extended as soon as Dan Bailey showed up."

Through more than half a century of the fight for clean rivers and public lands, leaders came and went but Dan Bailey was always there. He considered it a permanent project.

Each year someone receives a Dan and Helen Bailey Memorial Award, presented by a local committee for service in the Dan Bailey tradition.

Fly tiers of the early forties. Dan Bailey is at far end of the line. "Wall Fish" are of the old painted-in variety.

THREE

Where the Flies Are Made

There is romance at the fly tier's bench. In midwinter when slush ice whispers down the Yellowstone and there are cracking ice noises along the shallow Madison an intent young woman in Montana will remove her down jacket, adjust her vise and using hair and feathers from a long way off will make a delicate thing that will go to Norway, Argentina or New Zealand. Perhaps it is wanted for a certain fish in a certain pool. There is even a sort of romance in the feathers and fur that come from around the world to become an insect to deceive a trout in far places.

The patent office will not help to make a fly exclusive. Origins of thousands of fly patterns and their variations are obscured in time and geography. Many an "original" fly has acquired a name in one part of the country while a near-duplicate is called something completely different somewhere else.

Most flies are originated by amateurs, but the term "amateur" is not derogatory here for some of the world's finest tiers have never sold a fly in their lives. Although they might not be temperamentally suited to commercial fly making, most of the pattern originators do so in devising flies for their own use and work out the details through trial and error.

Most of the originators of famous flies are men, simply because most of the anglers are men. A famous fishing authority once stated that the best fly tiers are women who have never seen their product in use. Perhaps we should modify that to say that most of the best *production* fly tiers are women. There are men with powerful paws and thick fingers who can produce exquisite things, but most of them are not restricted by time and they are driven by the knowledge that if the fly is just right it will take fish — for themselves.

Some of the Bailey fly tiers at work after the Wall of Fame was made up of plaques.

Men seldom make good production fly tiers, whatever their ability. We'll leave it at that and put it down to the male temperament. They simply don't stay at it very long in most cases. Red Monical, who doesn't tie flies any more, says he could do it as well as ever except that his eyes aren't as good as they were. Perhaps the appeal of tying for the fun of seeing a fish take your creation can fade if you make enough flies. Dan Bailey, famous as one of the world's fly authorities and a truly expert tier himself, did not tie in his later years although he remained a judge of materials and the finished product.

Dan, of course, was allergic to most of the things used to make flies, as he was allergic to antelope and deer and the cattle on his ranch. He would laughingly complain about his problems with game and cattle but faced his daily work without mentioning it. When a trip to the Mayo Clinic revealed he was allergic to "almost everything in the business," some thought he would retire. He didn't, but there was a rule around the place that the floor should not be swept when Dan was working. After Dan died, Red said it seemed strange to have the floor swept in daytime.

Louise Monical, who heads the Dan Bailey fly-tying department, must be one of the world's greatest tiers but she is not famous for she doesn't cast her flies and she does not name them. She fills custom requests with uncanny accuracy and no one knows how many different patterns she has produced — or how many tiers she has trained, but there have been hundreds. A thousand? Now she spends more time at her desk than at a bench.

There are, of course, few tiers of her ability, but there could be some we have never heard of. The production worker is a special person, more so if he or she can produce new designs upon request. Call that custom tying. Fly making can be either an art form or a process of skilled production requiring an economy of movement and exactitude of construction that produces dozens of flies exactly alike as far as the fisherman can tell. Louise Monical can do both and not many can.

Experts can recognize the work of various tiers in many cases, even though several produce equally good flies, so perhaps even production tying is an art form.

Not everyone can become an expert. There was a time when Dan Bailey said it was time to train more workers and Louise responded that she had tried everybody in town who showed any interest.

Looking at a box of Number Twenty flies, which may not be harder to tie than bigger ones but are always more impressive in their delicacy, there is a recurring fantasy of bleachers set up along a classical stream when a hatch is at its peak. The bleachers would be filled with fly tiers who had never been fly fishing and they could watch an expert angler at work, could see the naturals being taken with gentle bulges and then could see their own flies disappear in the same kind of dimple, and then watch big trout feel the hook and come out in clean jumps. It might not make fisherwomen of them but any reaction would be exciting. Would some of them say, "So what?"

Louise says that about one-fourth of those who take up fly tying succeed to the extent that they work at it for considerable time. The problem, she says, can be a lack of manual dexterity, but it's a particular kind of dexterity and it is hard to define. Some women who are noted for fine sewing don't work out at the tying bench.

The number of Bailey tiers has fluctuated a great deal since there have been both full and part-time workers. When Louise Monical first began tying in 1947 she had been credit manager for a local Montgomery Ward store and had been attracted to what seemed to be strange going-ons at the fly shop. At that time the tying was done entirely by piecework and her first 48-hour week netted $20. There is a great deal of personnel turnover but the average tier of recent times has been with the store for more than ten years.

Developments in fly-tying equipment have been carefully tested and evaluated. In the early days there were no bobbins and tiers suffered from finger cuts until they could develop protective callouses. Bobbins not only saved fingers but made greater tension possible. The whip finisher was established as a tool before the bobbin.

There are few hazards but some workers have suffered shoulder trouble — not from extreme exertion but from holding the arm in an unchanging position for long periods. Red Monical, a tall man, used an extension welded to his vise.

In 1941 Dan Bailey had a catalog, printed 4" x 6" with 12 pages. It featured reverse-hackled flies, explaining how that sort of tie floated better and that was a continually featured development. No one can be credited with true invention of the method. Bailey's listing included an assortment of the Lee Wulff hairwings and Bailey's Bi Flies. The stone fly patterns were explained as "salmon and trout flies" since the Western names were "salmon flies" for the big naturals and "trout flies" for the smaller ones. There also were Fan Wings, Bi-Visibles, Spiders and Variants. The tapered fly leaders could be had either in Spanish gut or DuPont Nylon. At that time the gut leaders were still preferred by a large share of fly casters. When Bailey first arrived in Montana he had found most local fishermen using snelled wet flies, often with droppers.

The Muddler Minnow probably got Dan Bailey's Fly Shop as

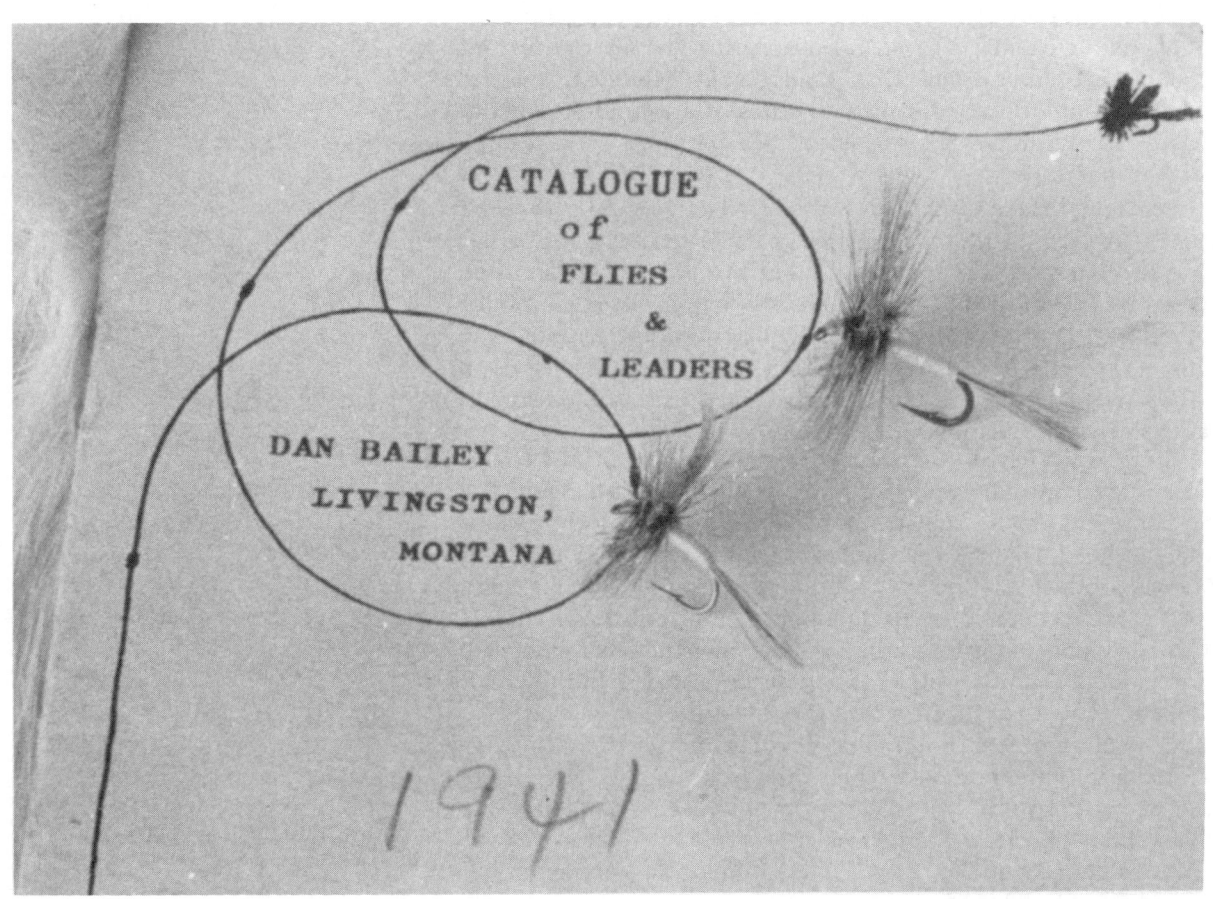

In 1941 Dan Bailey issued a small catalog. The two flies are "Dan Bailey Dry Flies" that came later and were discontinued because plastic bodies weren't durable.

much recognition as anything else it ever produced, and Dan Bailey didn't claim to have originated it. The man who did probably wouldn't mind that Bailey sold Muddlers by the thousands and modified it into all sorts of streamers — if the Muddler truly is a "streamer" instead of a dry fly — or "bass bug" for that matter.

According to Dan Gapen, his father Don first tied the Muddler in 1937 at Virgin Falls on the Nipigon River in Ontario. At that time the Nipigon was famous for big brook trout and Gapen knew they favored the "cockatush" or sculpin. The sculpin or cottus (still another name) was called a "muddler sculpin" and Gapen says the Muddler name stuck with the new fly. Don Gapen was a resort operator and descendant of an English and Scottish fly tying family.

When Bailey began to produce them some time in the fifties there were some variations from the original. At first glance the chief difference was a more closely cropped and tighter constructed head. From there the variations spread, and although Bailey's produce a "standard" Muddler, other tiers have gone to really fanciful variations, the burr head being about all that's left of the original. It was the right time for the Muddler for the use of streamers and other big flies had become stylish in the West. Public acceptance of the first Bailey Muddlers was immediate and fishermen seemed to think it was revolutionary.

Sitting on the porch of their ranch house, Helen Bailey watched young John Bailey ride by on a pony. His blond hair was close cropped in the current crew cut.

"We call him 'Muddler,'" said Helen. John doesn't remember it.

The basic Muddler Minnow, sometimes almost obscured by its progeny, was made mostly of natural deer hair and nearly matching turkey feather. The idea of a white one came up very shortly and at that time Vince Hamlin was famous as the artist of Alley Oop, syndicated comic strip of a caveman and his associates. Hamlin, who spent his summers fishing in Montana, had introduced a character called the Mizzoulian Spook, and that name went with the white Muddler.

In its different sizes and hues the Muddler thing spread to black bass water and the oceans. One famous angler announced that the small white one was the world's most productive trout catcher.

The Spruce Fly, famous itself as a trout streamer, was crossed with the Muddler Minnow and the Spuddler was the inevitable result. The Marabou Muddler came when someone fancied the crawly attraction of supple feather rather than the stiff minnow body. Some of Chester Marion's many colorful interpretations appear in recent catalogs.

It went on from there with Muddlers on the surface, on the bottom and in between as they are today. Probably no other fly has had as much publicity in magazines and books. Dave Whitlock once mentioned that the Muddler could be tied to represent a caddis fly, grasshopper, dace, sculpin, mayfly nymph or crayfish. Slowly sinking in a tidal creek of southern Florida it passes as a "glass minnow" that has been injured on the surface. It pops urgently on the surface in weedy largemouth water. Slightly altered, of course, it works where fish find swimming field mice or voles. Anyway, it looks alive, even if some models are simply the ancient "powder puff" with a short tail. Perhaps it is a system rather than just a fly. In 1959 and 60 it accounted for more than half of the big trout that were outlined on the Bailey walls.

There is a standard joke among the old timers that Red Monical married Louise because she could tie the Muddler Minnow well. The story goes that Louise quit her job at the shop and moved away and Dan told Red to get her back if he had to marry her. I doubt if the Muddler Minnow was the only factor in their happy marriage but it's a good story.

The Wulff series of hairwings was developed by Dan Bailey although he did not invent the hairwing concept. The originator was his old friend Lee Wulff, one of the best known of all fly fishermen, making outstanding catches of both salt and freshwater fish on fly rods. He is credited with the first fishing vest.

Wulff's idea of tying a hair wing was to imitate the Gray Drake of the Ausable and he also tied a white one. Through some sort of black magic, Wulff was able to tie flies rapidly without a vise and was fishing with Bailey on the Esopus in the winter of 1929-30 when he tried his creation and caught some 30 fish with it. Dan named it. The Wulffs, of course, are true impression flies (which Bailey always favored) and they float high. Best of all, they can be seen by the fisherman, even in the small sizes.

For some time in the Montana shop Dan tied all of the Wulffs himself. He introduced the grizzly and black ties. Red Monical came up with the Blonde Wulff. Also, there is the Royal Wulff, a Royal Coachman with hair wings instead of traditional feathers. Coachman flies, probably best known of all and tied in dozens of forms, got their name from a true royal coachman, Tom Bosworth, a famous angler who wielded a whip for British soverigns.

Patterns have come and gone — and a fly is very seldom really new — but some of those in recent Bailey catalogs have stood a test of time, beginning with Bailey and his associates. There are the Wulffs, of course, the Meloche, (a very light-colored mayfly imitation), Dan's Deer Hopper, John Bailey's Elk Hair Hopper, the variety of Muddlers and the Bi Fly. There is the Dark Spruce Fly (the original Light Spruce came from elsewhere) the Elk Hair Salmon Fly, originated by John Bailey, a Fresh Water Shrimp originated by Dan, and the Elk Hair Caddis and Little Brown

Caddis from Fred Terwilliger, a long time employee before he went into business for himself in West Yellowstone.

If there is a pattern of development it is the increased use of highly buoyant hair such as elk and deer hair for buoyance and durability.

The Bailey Dragon Fly is some 20 years old and the Mossbacks are imitations of stone fly nymphs in various shades. The Mossbacks use different tones on back and underside and have the flattened silhouette of the real thing.

Bailey's have a special version of the Silver Doctor streamer, although the original name is a very old one. They experimented endlessly with various Mylar-bodied streamers.

Early innovations that have been superseded by other patterns include the "Bear Family" of wet hair flies and a series of "creepers" in various colors. The Pop Eye (bead eyes) lost popularity with advent of modern sinking lines although similar flies persist in shad country. The grub and maggot flies caught a great many trout along with whitefish. There was a Woven Body Salmon Fly and the smaller Woven Trout Fly.

An early Dan Bailey Dry Fly, although effective, was discontinued because its plastic body was not durable enough.

Most custom flies have been supplied for orders of six or more in a given size and at a slight extra charge. Custom fly requests sometimes involved elaborate patterns a fisherman had read about and that were produced by authorities who had done so with no regard to the time spent. On the first order for such complexities the tiers try it but if it proves too expensive they must decline further orders lest they produce some hundred-dollar flies. Atlantic salmon flies, deep in tradition and exotic materials, are both expensive to provide and difficult to assemble. The word is out that some simple ties are generally just as good.

Without counting the various colors there are some 30 different materials regularly used for flies. At Bailey's dyeing fur and feathers was once a major task but less necessary as material sources have developed. Material purchasing requires a great deal of experience and judgment of feathers and hair is a craft in itself. The supplies have waxed and waned through the years, a shortage of one kind of cape eventually ending when demand caused the right kind of poultry to be provided.

Early in the game hackle feathers were supplied loose and sold by the pound. Later, they arrive in cape form, much easier for the tier to use since a row of hackle feathers is likely to be of about the same size and quality.

Use of dry flies gradually increased in the West although most Easterners felt only the big ones would be needed. Joe Brooks probably did more than any other fisherman to promote the use of streamers. The big ones he used, such as the double-tied

Flies originated by Dan Bailey's
Top, left to right: Olive Shrimp, Dark Spruce Fly, Dan Mayfly Nymph (olive.)
Second from top: Silver Doctor Streamer, Elk Hair Caddis, Missoulean Spook.
Third from top: Meloche, Spuddler, Elk Hair Salmon Fly.
Fourth from top: Yellow Marabou Muddler, Little Brown Caddis, Black Wulff, Light Mossback, Brown, Green & White Mylar Streamer.
Second from bottom, left: Dan's Deer Hopper.
Bottom: Dragon Fly, Yellow Bi-Fly, John's Elk Hair Hopper.

Blondes, caught big fish, especially for long casters — and the long cast became important. Then there were many more big flies, some of them duplicates of salt water patterns.

There are times when the fly makers wonder a little about the people out there who use their product. A recent complaint concerned a "dry" fly that the customer couldn't make float, and he returned his order twice. It was finally concluded that he was not using dry fly flotant of any kind. Almost any "dry" fly will sink eventually if nothing is applied to it.

And the breaking hook problem is an ancient one with fly manufacturers. On rare occasions a small barb is broken by a tier and not noticed, but most of the breaks occur when the caster tics a rock on his backcast. He discovers it when he has lost a fish. Dan Bailey mildly consoled complaining customers on many occasions.

"It may be the hook broke on the fish." he would say, "but I believe most of our hooks can be straightened without breaking. In nearly every case a broken one has struck a rock on a backcast."

Usually the explanation satisfied the customer.

But people must be satisfied before the fish are.

"Fly collections are 90% for the ego and 10% for the fish," Dan said, but he recognized the pride in perfection.

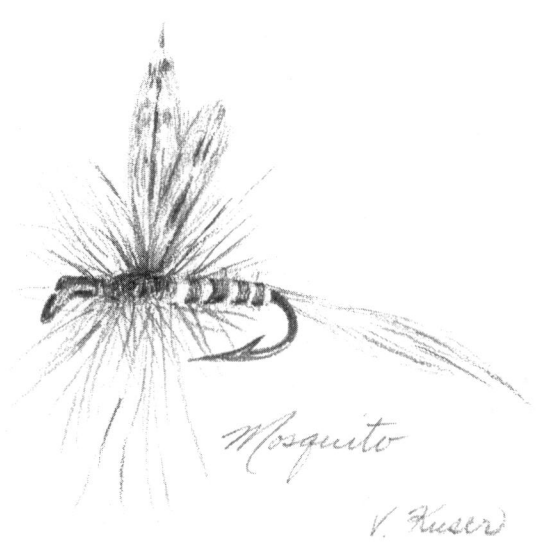

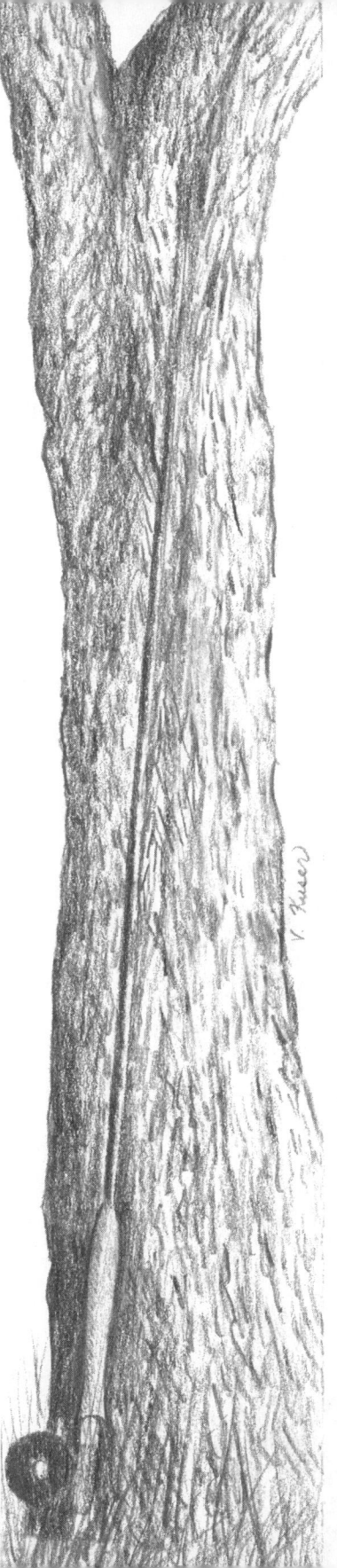

FOUR

Tackle Matters

He liked fine tackle but would have fished if he'd had only a willow stick. When Dan Bailey died there was some question about his "collection of rods."

What was left were mostly good, practical rods, but not particularly collector's items, and there were no true antiques. At one time or another he'd owned some personal gems but he was generous with them.

"He must have given most of them away," said John Bailey as he surveyed Dan's estate.

On one trip with Dan I saw him using what I considered a very unusual bamboo and I believe it was an Edwards *Quadrate*, a 4-strip model that has lasted through the years, now something of a novelty. Square rods are different.

At any rate the one Dan produced had an extremely slow action and it wasn't well suited for the kind of fishing we were doing at the time. He just brought it to see how it worked in wind and big water, I guess. He'd appeared with unusual rods before and after trying a few casts with it I dismissed it from mind. Then, many years later, I was digging up some rod history and needed a picture of a 4-stripper. I remembered the Edwards.

Oh, yes, Dan said he was pretty sure he remembered that rod, but he thought he didn't have it any more. He disappeared from his living room and made a search. Maybe it was at the store. It wasn't.

"I think I gave that rod away," Dan finally said apologetically. "Strange action, wasn't it?"

Being a bit absent-minded, Dan occasionally forgot to put his rod in the car for a short trip. He made one trip without much tackle of any kind and borrowed all sorts of junk to save the day.

Several times he mentioned that it was one of the best day's fishing he ever had. He caught a lot of trout and some of them were pretty big. This is just a little strange in view of the fact that surveys show how using fine equipment is one of the main incentives for skilled fishermen.

Favorite rods? Sure there were some, and they came from a variety of builders. The last two I remember his discussing were a C.W. Jenkins Bamboo for a Five line and little glass Winston for a Four. Perhaps it is unfair to mention these two when there were others from other famous makers, but by coincidence I owned one of the little Winstons and my wife got a Jenkins on Dan's recommendation. He used an Orvis Battenkill for many years. Dan chose his rods by their performance for his casting rather than because of their materials. His reels were both British and American.

In fishing big water Dan tended to carry a great deal of line in the air, probably because that was the way he fished a double-tapered line and the method carried over into weight-forward lines for heavy fishing. He tended toward a fairly wide loop and when he went to salt water he stayed with it. On his last trip to the Everglades we were a little worried about him.

He was using a good-sized streamer and he appeared to lay it on the water with considerable slack. Then he would appear to take up part of it by lifting his rod tip, a practice not recommended for salt water fish. Fishing was very slow that trip and we thought it essential that he have the best possible chance at any strike. Debie whispered to me that she didn't see how Dan was going to catch a fish like that and maybe we should help him a little. Since I had discussed such problems with him many years before, I didn't feel like approaching the subject again so I didn't. A short while later a big snook boiled out of the mangroves and Dan hooked and landed it — somehow. It had to be luck. Then a second fish came out and Dan bit his pipestem and hooked and landed it too. Okay.

I do not know if it was good for business or not, but Dan was insistent upon selling fishermen what they needed — and only what they needed. Roger Powalisz, Bailey's friend for many years, said that Dan took as much interest in selling a kid a few split shot as he did in supplying the expedition needs of experts.

Bailey would have fished if he'd had only a handline.

"Then a second fish came out and Dan bit his pipestem and hooked and landed it too. Okay."
(Dan Bailey with a snook caught in the Everglades.)

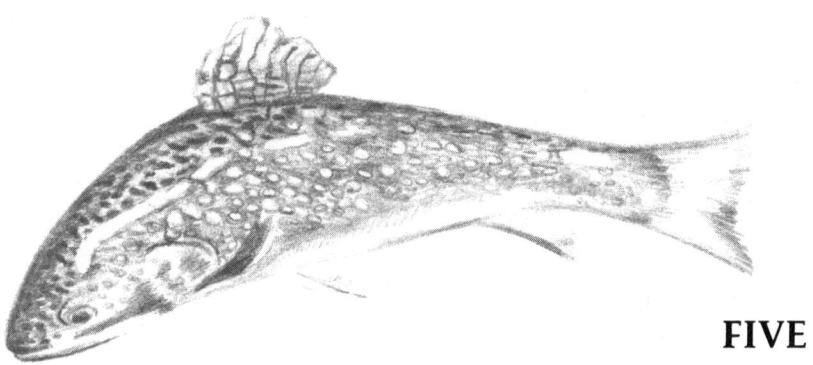

FIVE

The Tank Fish

The "tank fish" was almost as important as the wall fish in early promotion of the Bailey store. The tank fish lived in an aquarium against the front window (and sometimes still does) to be viewed by passersby. The tank fish, a sizable trout, was viewed pensively by fishermen, who guessed its weight, and by non-fishermen, who admired its spots.

The tank fish mortality rate is fairly high — not as high, I hasten to add, as mortality rates in the wild. Watched over by the entire corps of employees and offered plenty of selected food, the tank fish gets corpulant and blase'.

For many years the tank gave a little trouble now and then. You see it is located where air temperatures vary considerably and viewers from the inside had a tendency to lean against it for a better view of the tank fish, which sometimes carried names given to it by the Bailey people.

In the early days of the tank there would be a leak from time to time, the tank water sliding quietly under the feet of the fly tyers, who would spread the alarm. Trouble with the tank was a true emergency to Dan Bailey and the top priority was to get the fish to the nearby river before it suffered harm.

The first time we encountered John and Dorothy McDonald, the Baileys' close New York friends, I thought they acted a little strangely. We didn't know who they were and they were at Armstrong's Spring Creek where John fished diligently and Dorothy stood at attention nearby with a bucket. Since very few spring creek fishermen carried buckets instead of creels and hardly any of them employed caddys, I pondered over this until I learned John was on a diligent search for a tank fish. For the moment, the tank had no fish and the drill was to catch a trout of considerable size, pop it into a bucket of creek or river water and dash for the store.

Debie's first wallfish was caught on the evening of a tank fish incident. It was so late we assumed the store would be closing so we made haste toward the Bailey ranch. Speed was essential since the fish weighed exactly four pounds and one ounce and a little drying out might put it below the magic figure. This craze for a wallfish was a little silly and would be scorned today but we'd heard a lot about wallfish. After Debie's brown trout was hung it developed that it was the first woman's *stream* fish to be put on the wall.

When we arrived at Bailey's house Dan wasn't home yet. We rushed the trout to the scales (always kept at Bailey's in case of emergency) and found that it really did go four pounds and something less than an ounce. We left it on the scale platform and waited for Dan. As I recall, we stayed for dinner.

Dan was quite late in getting in. First, he grinned happily at Debie's fish. Then he mentioned that there had been some excitement at the store. Helen was fixing dinner.

"The tank broke again," Dan said, "but I got the fish to the river while he was still in good shape. Sure was lucky I was there."

Dan paused to get himself a drink.

"This time the tank broke out through the front window," Dan continued. "The water, glass and fish went all over the sidewalk and out into the street but I think it's pretty well cleaned up now and I got hold of the insurance people."

Dan got his pipe started.

"Oh, yes," he said. "I meant to tell you that there was a man standing on the sidewalk looking at the fish when the window broke out."

Helen dropped a pan.

"My God! Is he all right?"

"He seems to be all right," Dan said. "I wiped him off and couldn't find anything wrong. But I guess he was surprised. He acted a little nervous. The fish is all right. I got it to the river pretty fast."

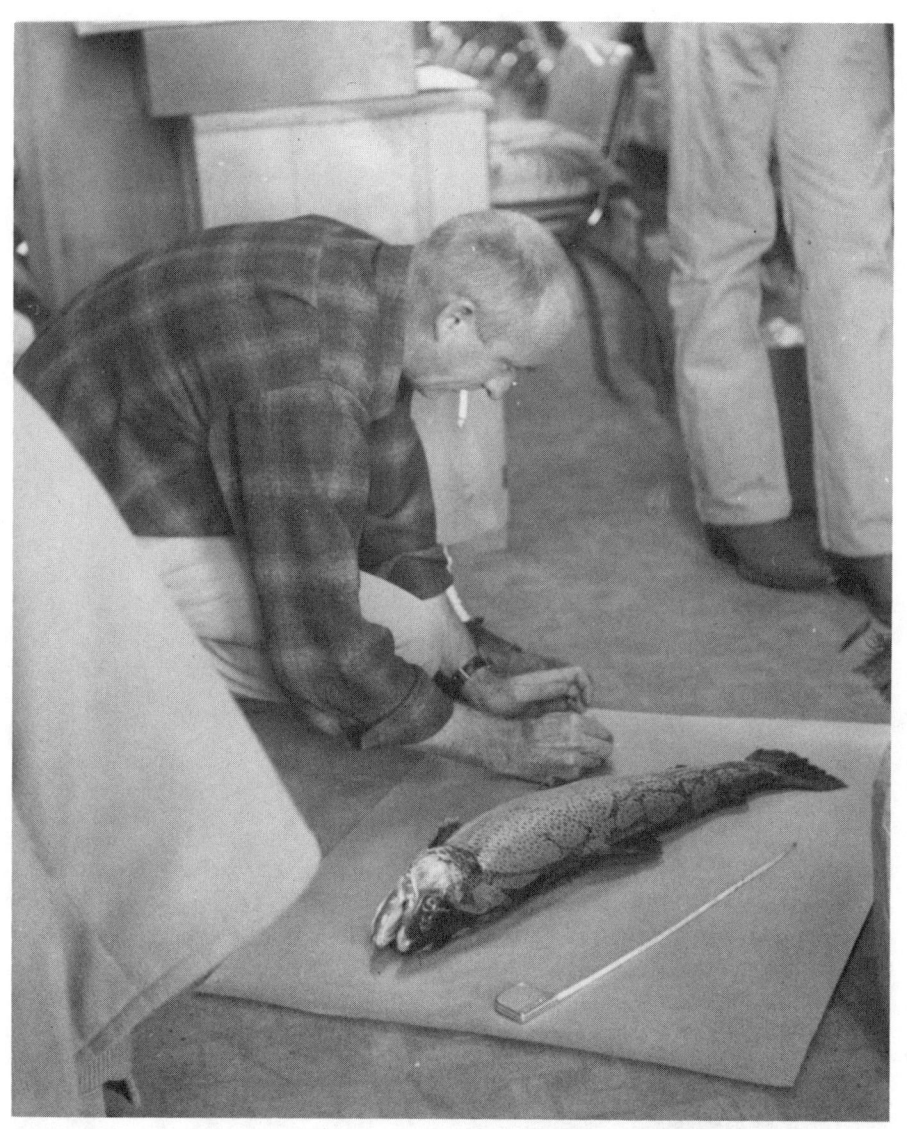

Red Monical outlines a trout for the Wall of Fame.

Dan Bailey's allergy keeps him at a distance while young John dresses an antelope.

SIX

Hunting Trips

Dan was a good hunter, even though he didn't seem to work at it. Helen and Dan Bailey laughed so much about hunting that you could easily get the wrong impression that Dan was a sort of maladroit where guns and mountains were concerned.

The hunting jokes began with Dan's allergy toward deer, antelope and other kinds of hairy things. Once Dan had a deer down he'd begin sneezing and his eyes would water. In the case of deer or antelope it was a joke, but Dan owned some cattle before he found out he was allergic to them too. Perhaps that made it easier for the Baileys to leave their beloved ranch and move a few miles into Livingston. Peter Fonda, the actor, has owned the place recently.

Incidentally, Dan finally found he was allergic to most fly tying materials but refused to let that interfere with business. That was his firm contact with fishing.

Dan had done considerable hunting before he went to Montana and when he got there he really went after the deer, elk and antelope while times were hard — and later on, when the grocery bill was not such an ogre, Helen insisted on wild meat for the freezer. She cooked wild meat perfectly and continually urged Dan into the hills during hunting season.

I think Dan's favorite hunting was for deer in the mountains although he never said it in so many words. He would hunt ducks, ruffed and blue grouse and sage hens. He would rather fish. For that matter, Dan liked to play bridge and he enjoyed photography, at which he was pretty good. He would rather fish.

He was a rather deliberate shot with a rifle and had considerable knack with a pistol. Of course he engaged in considerable gun business at the store, but the technical details of shooting did not interest him in the slightest. Dramatically shown an expensive shotgun of exotic make he once became just a little irked.

"It's just a gun!" Dan said. "It is just a gun! It is not like a rod. It is just a gun!"

But he took the little sting from his words when he laughed apologetically toward the gun's owner.

"I just don't care anything about guns!" he said, and went back to his desk.

"The main thing about hunting," he said to me, "is to get the meat in the locker so we can go fishing. Often this is possible on the same day if I get up early."

But at times he was trophy conscious. When they lived on the ranch Dan made a short hunting trip and stayed far into the night. When he finally came out he was carrying the head and antlers of a spectacular mule deer. This upset Helen, who was interested in venison rather than antlers. The meat was left in the mountains overnight and she worried about it.

"I could have killed him," she said, a frequent remark concerning Dan's hunting. It was almost a term of endearment.

Early in their Montana residence the Baileys decided to butcher an elk in their kitchen, which was freshly painted a gleaming white. The meat cutting altered the decor considerably.

"Even the ceiling was spattered," Helen said. Dan laughed.

Dan told his hunting stories as he did most of his fishing stories, with what I considered dramatic understatement.

His prize buck, for example:

"I was hunting and I met this big deer walking through the woods so I shot it."

And the rather grim episode in which a wounded bull elk charged Dan and chased him around a tree.

"He would chase me and when I got ahead of him I would stop and shoot him some more," Dan explained.

Dan was a fine hunting companion all right, but he had one fault — a carefree attitude about the difficulties in getting game out of the mountains. Most hunters who operate on upended ground give great thought to the drag trail and pulling a 200-pound buck is best done downhill. Dan tried to get them while uphill all right, but time of day was not important. The reason became simple with a little thought. You could drag a deer at night when Dan did not care to fish. If he finally got a deer late in the evening he might save a whole day of fishing.

On the trips I made with him, Dan invariably came back to camp or truck last of the party. The sight of him carrying a deer liver in gathering darkness made Red Monical light his cigarette nervously. Dan invariably explained that the deer would be quite easy to get out, that he had it well marked and that it was all a downhill drag. Even in the night he'd find it again. I'll concede that. This was a little unusual for a fellow who regularly got lost along a trout stream — and didn't care.

This nocturnal deer-liver fetching, coupled with Dan's proclivity for testing automobiles as all-terrain vehicles has led to some memorable adventures, one of the more graphic of which occurred on the American Fork River some distance from the store. After leaving the ranch and moving to town, Dan preferred to hunt some distance away from Livingston, and preferably in a new area. His attitude at the top of a new ridge must have been similar to that of Lewis and Clark.

There were five of us on the American Fork trip, exactly the number of hunters finally needed. Of course we did not know we were going to the American Fork and on the way we passed a beautiful marshy lake covered with ducks. In the intervening years Red Monical, a chronic duck hunter, has always wondered where the lake was. Besides Dan, Red and me there were John Bailey and a high school friend of his, both of a fitting age for what they were about to do.

The vehicle was a recently introduced model of van (long before people painted landscapes on them) and Dan had used it for a couple of years without a tuneup — a monument to the manufacturer's expertise. Dan did not deliberately avoid checkups but he did not like to have his cars tied up at a shop when they might be needed suddenly for emergency fishing.

"Don't go downhill very far with this, Father," said John (we called him Johnny then). "It won't come back up!"

"Oh, I think it will be all right," Dan said mildly in the same tone he used when playing his version of Russian roulette with a nearly empty gas tank as he passed service station after service station on long trips.

"This looks like a good place," Dan finally said, somewhat after midday, and headed the van (or was it *station wagon* then?) over the brow of a near-precipice and down a steep jeep trail that seemed to descend endlessly into a canyon.

"Don't, Father!" cried Johnny, "It won't come back up! It *can't* come back up!"

"Oh, I think it might," Dan said through the almost measurable tension in the back seat. "We'll see."

At bottom of the canyon we found a level parking place and gathered our rifles and other gear while Johnny stared apprehensively back the way we had come, being very quiet for a teenager. We had not seen another vehicle for miles and heard only the wind in the pines.

We separated and Dan went off in that short, even stride that had always gone so well in the mountains. He was out of sight almost instantly and with hardly a sound. For a moment I helped Johnny look back up the hill and then took to my own chosen ridge where I walked softly the rest of the day and saw only a giant snowshoe rabbit that stared at me like some backwoods Harvey before he hopped courteously off the pine-needled game trail.

I came back well before dusk, sighting the green van from some distance, and within a few minutes four of us were there, only Dan missing. No one had killed a deer. Red began to gather firewood and I wondered why. I should have known.

"This," said Red, "is to keep us from freezing to death while we're waiting for Dan."

Late fall chill closed in, almost tangibly, and soon it was barely light enough to shoot.

"I wish it was darker," Red said. "He still could kill something and I'll bet he will!"

Johnny looked back up the hill.

The single shot came then, bounced about the slopes and peaks, booming dully.

"I knew it!" Red said, and went for more wood. Soon it was dark the way it gets dark in late fall at the bottom of a canyon.

When Dan appeared with a minor rustling in the buckbrush at the edge of the fire's glow, he was carrying a deer liver in a plastic bag. He lighted his pipe and said the deer was "right up there" on a little ridge. Easy to get down, he said.

He led us off into the darkness and Johnny and his friend followed his directions well ahead until they found the buck lying on the ridge. In a welcome bit of youthful showoff, they rolled and dragged it most of the way down before we got there. We then dragged it to the van and the smoldering fire and loaded it into the van.

"It won't go back up there," John said.

We pushed and heaved and we finally went out by a rather unusual method which you might need if you ever get stuck in a canyon with an underpowered vehicle. Each of four of us would take a rock the size of a loaf of bread and stand by. Dan would open the suffering engine to an erratic scream and slip the clutch. As the van lunged and died, each of the rest of us would slam a rock behind a wheel.

During most of the ascent Dan had apparently been sucking on a cold pipe. Now he filled and lighted it.

"I wonder how it would be to go over to the Clark's Fork this time of year and use some big streamers," he said above the wheezing breaths of his collapsed crew. Red Monical was breathing hard and I am not sure what he said.

Dan's rifle, at the time I used to hunt with him, was a 270 bolt action, and by that time some of his youthful excitement had dissipated because he took great pains to collect his venison and antelope with as little meat loss as possible. Still, he paid little attention to the equipment. There was the time over on the Madison when several of us reached the mountains before dawn, hoping to intercept bucks moving up from the river bottom at daylight.

There weren't many of them that morning and we separated to hunt along some foothill ridges. I was next to Dan, but some distance away, and I heard him shoot once— then again, and then in a series of about 20 shots. They were in a measured cadence and I could visualize no situation that would cause so much gunfire. Then I heard young Johnny calling across a ravine. Johnny wanted to know what was going on.

He had a deer located in plain sight, Dan said, and he couldn't hit it. He pointed it out to Johnny, I guess. Anyway, there was a single lighter report from Johnny's 243, the deer was down and Johnny began working his way over to help Dan dress it out.

Later that day we examined Dan's rifle and found that something had knocked his scope sight so badly out of line he could not have hit a parking lot.

"Somewhere on that mountain," Dan mused, "I was shooting a 2-inch group."

When Dan acquired his heart problem the doctor told him to avoid strenuous exercise.

"He told me not to drag any deer," Dan said. "I guess somebody will have to go with me."

Dan interpreted the instructions very literally. He would obey the doctor and he would not drag a deer. This, as he accepted it, did not mean he could not climb precipitous cliffs or rush about the mountains in order to collect venison so that he could get back to fishing.

Dan, Johnny and I parked Bud Schlect's jeep at the foot of Bangtail Ridge. I don't recall why we had Bud's jeep when Bud wasn't along. About the time we reached the foot of the ridge it began to snow — huge flakes that promised more to come, and I was in almost as big a hurry as Dan.

"If I get a deer, I'll have to call on you," Dan told me. "The doctor told me not to drag one, you know."

Dan went up the ridge with short, stabbing steps, disappearing in the snow. Johnny had already left at a different angle. I chose a route of my own and had worked my way to what I considered the proper altitude and was just beginning to hunt my area, knowing any game would be seen at close range, when Dan's 270 thumped off there, its report deadened by snowfall.

"Charl-e-e-e-e!" he called a moment later, drawing out the name so that it would not have been recognizable if I hadn't known what it was.

I answered obediently and began working my way toward Dan and his deer. I pushed and dragged it to the jeep while Dan carried the rifles and kept up a stream of apology for interfering with my hunt. We left the dressed deer at the jeep and went off in planned directions again.

It took me about 20 minutes to once more get into hunting territory but everybody had two deer tags that season and Dan's rifle thumped again.

"Charle-e-e-e!"

With the second deer dragged to the jeep somewhere around noon, Dan smiled, thanked me profusely and said there might be time for a little fishing that afternoon. Since I could see only a few feet through the snowfall, I doubted that. Anyway, it was sometime that day that Johnny killed a really big buck, doing most of the dragging and all of the dressing himself with teenage enthusiasm.

Helen was delighted with all of the venison.

On some occasions, Dan took the opening day of deer season as a time of exploration, expertly steering a 4-wheel drive into areas where he usually admitted, after becoming hopelessly lost, that he had never been before. I did not like to follow Dan with a 4-wheel drive.

All of the time that I knew them the Baileys kept Labrador retrievers, a procession of pleasant rogues that never really did get to do much hunting. One of the most notable was Bozo, an ebony giant who leaped through wooden doors when confined. Much later was a procession of Labs which Dan allowed to wade with him when he fished (I guess Bozo did too), even though a frolicking Lab might cause some apprehension among skittish trout.

On one occasion a swarm of sage grouse descended on an area where we were hunting antelope. Dan took his shotgun from the truck and gathered a limit of the big birds to the ecstacy of the current Labrador, which probably wondered where such joyous retrieving opportunities had been all her life.

Dan loved to hunt. Perhaps only the fact that he liked fishing better kept him from covering the world with his rifle.

"On one occasion when a swarm of sage grouse descended on an area where we were hunting antelope Dan took his shotgun from the truck and gathered a limit . . ."

SEVEN

Away From Home

Dan Bailey was a lot of fun away from home. He approached any new kind of fishing with enthusiasm and modesty and looked at a new species of fish as if he had found a pearl in a restaurant oyster.

For some years we had tried to get Dan and Helen to Florida and when it finally worked out I went to rather unusual preparations. Here was a guy who had steered us through the best of Montana fishing and had never been introduced to snook or tarpon, the specialties of the mangrove Everglades country. We kept a house trailer at Everglades City, backed up to a seawall at what was then called the Everglades Small Boat Dock, run by Ted Smallwood, one of the famous guides of mangrove coast fishing.

We had two aluminum boats ready for the Bailey visit. One, a spare, stood on a trailer by the dock, just in case of motor trouble with the other. We were covering all bets. Major outboard repair wasn't too speedy at Everglades City in those days.

Before Dan and Helen were to arrive we slipped into a small bay with two brackish feeder creeks. There had often been small tarpon at the mouth of one and I slid the boat up to it while Debie measured line for a careful cast. The streamer landed just right and as she began her retrieve there was a great, silent swirl. No strike, but the fish was there. If anyone can tiptoe with a pair of 8-foot oars, I did it getting away from that fish. Then we found another tarpon at another creek and left it alone too — or was that a big snook? The swirl was pretty broad.

The Baileys' flight got into Miami late at night and we headed across Florida along the deserted Tamiami Trail highway. It was warm and humid — warm even for South Florida just after

Christmas. We stopped somewhere while crossing the "river of grass" and got out of the car to listen to the pulsating sounds of the Everglades night, the almost startling cacophony of calls from insects, reptiles, birds and animals. It always frightens me a little to step from a car into the sub-tropical blackness and to hear so many things I do not really recognize. Helen and Dan thought it was great but there was ice on the dock back of the trailer next morning. It was the only time I have seen ice there and I hadn't really believed the weather forecast. We'd try anyway.

I guess the cold hadn't had time to really chill the water. Anyway, the fish were ready to entertain visitors the next day. Dan caught ladyfish until he said he believed some of them were coming around the second time. He hooked and lost innumerable small tarpon and Helen, who had never claimed to be much of an angler, caught one from the bank on a highway shoulder to Dan's delight. Finally, he landed one himself. He caught snook and jack crevalle and spotted weakfish and he approached it all with wide-eyed delight. That's the kind of company to have on your favorite fishing waters.

He was intrigued by the fast retrieve managed by salt water fishermen. Hadn't needed that on trout, he said, so he learned it.

Then, one other time Helen and Dan visited the Everglades. That time the boat was more comfortable and we were all very noticeably older. Dan and I went down to Shark River with Ted Smallwood, running outside in considerable sea, and Ted used his customary heavy hand on the throttle of his over-powered 17-footer. We touched down only occasionally in some of the rougher spots and when I found myself airborne from the front seat I would be on the same level with Dan, who grinned broadly.

Dan caught fish but I felt he would have had a good time if he hadn't. In fact, I don't recall any serious complaint of his about fishing. Very poor fishing usually left him with a sort of musing wonderment about *why* it was poor.

Dr. Jim Smith, the Livingston dentist, Dan and I went up to Duck Lake near Glacier National Park. At that time there were some really big rainbows being caught there and our expectations were pretty high. We pulled a boat behind my old Surburban and fishing was slow. Smith, an excellent angler, caught the only two fish we landed and did it on the first day. We tried hard the second day but quit a little early because of a storm that roared out of the mountains and tossed our boat unhappily. No strikes at all.

On the long drive back to Livingston Dan sat between Jim and me, evidently lost in deep thought. The truck had been rigged so that there was no back seat. Smith and I carried on a conversation across Dan, who seemed to hear none of it at all. At intervals, there would be a pause in the discussion, whereupon Dan would state:

"I can't understand why we had *no strikes at all today.*"
No complaint, Just wonderment. He said it several times.

" . . . Helen, who had never claimed to be much of an angler, caught one (tarpon) from the bank on a highway shoulder to Dan's delight."

"On a small and unknown creek your whole day can be a little fragile. A duck can change it."

EIGHT

The Little Creeks

Besides the famous streams whose seemingly unlimited trout are capable of staring down thousands of fly casters every year, there are a number of smaller and lesser-known ones, many of them having only local names. They are not expensive but they are not introduced to the multitudes for they can stand only limited pressure, being too narrow or too shallow.

Only a literary boor would write of "secret" creeks by name and I don't know of many. They may be on private property or in national forests or on BLM land, and either this fishing is exclusive or it doesn't exist. Dan Bailey fished a few of these creeks that he had found himself, doing it ruefully because he knew most of his customers couldn't find them. It made him feel a little guilty, he said.

On a small and unknown creek your whole day can be a little fragile. A duck can change it. A lady bluewinged teal can be a nuisance. A hen mallard can be a catastrophe. These things are likely to happen along in Montana's August. The ducklings have hatched and they have ideal homes along many of the little creeks. Not many fishermen. The duck nests are in the clumps of weeds and grass that, for one reason or another, are not bothered by livestock.

It's a good midsummer day, just a little overcast from time to time. A few caddis flies and an occasional mayfly show up along the creek — much better than on those days when flies hatch in swarms and come down the current, almost in a mat of frail wings and bodies. On those frustrating days the slothful trout lie near the surface like indolent panhandlers and roll sloppily among the flies. At such times the most artfully dressed and doped artificial on the most hairlike tippet is taken only by accident along with the naturals. But such days don't occur often. On our day, things are just right.

You peer at the curling currents from a distance and then a fish shows a blunt trout nose as well as fins and tail. They're taking surface things or things so near the surface that a dry fly should be a happy choice. Nymphs, especially deep ones, are poor choices here for there's too much vegetation to tangle them in midsummer.

You walk around and downstream, stumbling along through heavy grass, weeds and brush for there are no paths or picnic benches. You get some 50 yards below one of the best spots where the fish have bunched up in a bend, and only then do you ease your way into the water, clinging to overhanging weeds.

At that point there is a clattering splatter and a stentorian squawk of horror. It is a brood of young mallards and their noisy mother, the ducklings half swimming and half flying upstream, having swarmed out of the shoreline grass near where you stepped in. The hen does the crippled bird act with a verve to shame any overacting human tragedian. She flails the water, stirring mud along the edge, crosses the creek to make sure you see her and splashingly follows her offspring around the bend where the fish had been rising, then turns off to one side and disappears.

It is quiet again and you can hear a pheasant rooster cackling brokenly in a strand of cottonwoods. There is no sign of rising fish in the bend. If a neighborly muskrat had cruised through them they would have moved away with gentle swells but a terrified mallard mother is different. She is spreading an alarm. You might as well wait, for the fish have disappeared.

It's 10 minutes later when a fish shows again in the bend and it's a furtive rise near the bank, but all is well now, so you dope the Number Sixteen Caddis and stretch a minor kink from the upper section of your leader. You begin to wade gently toward casting range but the mama duck is not satisfied.

Now why she comes back, I am not sure. Perhaps she thinks you are trailing her brood. A cautious wader stalking fish, I suppose, may appear to stalk a bunch of little ducks if you are a nervous duck mother. Anyway, the hen decides she may not have given a convincing performance the first time so she does the whole thing again, hammering her supposedly damaged wings across the area the fish would like to feed in.

Now on a short creek this business can continue for most of your fishing time and a dozen wing performances are not unusual. Multiply that total by the number of mallard families on a creek and there is a tendency to reconsider funds previously donated to Ducks Unlimited.

But there are days when the ducks are quiet except for occasional startled quacks as they come upon you unexpectedly while sliding in for a landing, the broods staying wherever they stay when they're out of sight.

Dan Bailey thought it was very funny to drive a hundred miles and have much of his fishing ruined by mallard thespians. He'd laugh and count the broods. But then, even on a hidden treasure of a trout stream when everything else was just right, Dan felt his Labrador had as much right to wade as he had — and if the Lab behaved very well he'd throw a stick or two for it as he left.

"It was a freestyle structure built by
a group with varying tastes . . . . . . but
no one took it very seriously."

NINE

The Hunting Lodge

There are hundreds of little foothill creeks like Bangtail, but it has a catchy name and we called it "Bangtail Country."

We built the cabin for deer hunting, not for fishing, but Dan was more interested in the trout than the deer, collecting his annual bucks with pleasure but with attention to the glistening little creeks seen through the willows and the cottonwoods. Although it was legal to shoot does in those days Dan always shot bucks, even though the does needed thinning. It was a concession to popular opinion. Many Montanans associated does with motherhood, the flag and general integrity.

At the time the other members of the Bangtail cabin group were on a big-fish run. There had been a turn to big rods and big brown trout in the late fall, using great flies and nymphs that Dan sold but didn't use a great deal. We built the cabin in a place hard to reach in wet or snowy weather, but where an occasional mule deer would study the new structure with amazement.

It was a freestyle structure built by a group with varying tastes, and since the man working on the back might have different ideas from the one driving nails at the front there was something to please and offend all concerned, but no one took it very seriously. Since I lacked all aptitude for the true carpentry, I volunteered to do the sawing. Give me a mark on a board and I'd try to follow it, and could do so to meet the rather inexact requirements. Jack Ward also served as a sawyer, denying the carpentry expertise he later revealed.

As the structure wandered over a fairly steep sage slope, the builders' individualities began to appear more and more. The disagreement concerning the amount of roof overhang was obvious in the finished structure since the roof's bare rafters extended far past the wall on one side. It had been decided to cut them later to fit whatever size roof was agreed upon. I can't remember whether they were ever shortened or not.

Since construction funds were extremely limited there was a premium on scrounging and various sharp dealings that the individuals would never have considered except in such a community project. When the jeep road was dry there were truckloads of strange materials unloaded at the site, some of them brought by large-eyed people discharging strange debts to members of the hunting group. Along toward the last I realized that part of the builders were more interested in the construction than in later residence. Freestyle architecture has a special appeal for frustrated building contractors engaged in some other livelihood — a sort of escape valve.

Dan never took a very active part in the construction, usually sending John to do his share. Johnny Bailey was invaluable because he was young enough that all of us ordered him about and he became a sort of assistant to everybody. Dan happily contributed his share of assessments, which never totaled more than the price of a box of 270 cartridges.

We had a double floor although such insurance was not in the original discussion. I do not recall any actual plans other than some scratched in the dirt — no, come to think of it, there were some paper diagrams but each carpenter used his own. Anyway, the double floor came about when Red Monical and Kenny Spalding were building the roof and dropped something. What they dropped went throught the original floor and it seemed easier to make another one over the fractured original. That made the cabin warmer anyway.

Since the hill sloped considerably and leveling plans had not been made until we were well under way, the cabin sloped. I believe it was Red who suggested we put the door near the bottom of the slope to facilitate sweeping or scrubbing. This worked beautifully although it was difficult to keep the door closed. It blew open once during a blizzard in small hours of the morning and Jack Ward yelled for Red to close it. Red sprang from his sleeping bag, half conscious, faced the storm in his long johns and was shiveringly back in his bag before he realized what had happened. Then he addressed Ward on the subject but Ward appeared to be asleep.

It was in the furnishings that things got out of hand. Everyone was to bring discarded furniture and other appointments and we got more than we really needed, the finished interior putting Holiday Inn to shame and including overstuffed things that had been noble works in their day. The enormous and gleaming kitchen range would now cause mayhem among antique collectors. The furnishing went on and on. Then the place was

decorated with mounted deer antlers from all over the area. Some of them were treasures.

We killed some really fine bucks from that cabin, Red actually getting one deer from the door, as I recall. We gradually learned the area, but the cabin itself was on private land. When the land sold we were ordered off, and although the new owners offered us an opportunity to salvage the cabin's furnishings, we simply didn't do it. With loss of the site we lost interest in the project and postponed getting anything from it until it was too late — I guess.

That cabin was located near National Forest land and it was in an area of abandoned homesteads. Some of the old ranch buildings had been pretty solid and could have been cleaned up and patched for our use, but at the time everybody wanted to build a cabin. A non-member of our little association asked me why we didn't just use an old ranch building and I had no satisfactory answer.

Anyway, Dan used the cabin for fishing more than for hunting and it was 20 years later that I got around to fishing the nearby creeks. I had to get to them from another road and although Ward kept telling me where the cabin was located from there I never did really understand. The gates were locked anyway.

The creeks were largely beaver pond water and hard to fish because the willows were thick and other brush was crowded in. Hunting for ruffed grouse along Bangtail I looked off a high bank and saw some 10-inch trout, remembered that Dan had fished there and decided to try it the following summer. Jack Ward saw the fish too.

The next summer I flipped a hairwing fly into the shallow little run below the big bank and the Number Five line fell on the placid surface like a hawser. Only tiny puffs of bottom mud showed where the trout had been. I had to do better than that.

So I worked my way through the willows to a leaky beaver dam that held water over my hip boots. This time I crouched a little and checked for backcast room. The cast went only 20 feet but the fly landed in the little pond's center and two 9-inch cutthroats squirted out from somewhere and one of them went down with my Wulff. I did such things a number of times that afternoon and flushed a ruffed grouse to be remembered the coming fall. I told Ward about it.

Jack has this creek fisherman's trick of wading in above a tiny pool and stirring a little mud. When it comes down to the fish they are ready to feed. Evidently they think it's raining upstream, although the mud could be caused by a cow cooling off or a beaver on an endless series of projects. Anyway, the fish strike when the haze of mud clouds their pool. Jack caught bigger fish than I did and he went back several times. But then he's a small-creek lover, same as Dan was. For that matter I can't think of any kind of creek Dan didn't like.

"The creeks were largely beaver pond water and hard to fish because the willows were thick and other brush was crowded in."

"Anyway, the Western fisherman equipped for anything that happens will have good chest waders and some kind of soles that will cling to impossible boulders."

TEN

Rod, Reel and Fly

A fly rod is a fly rod in Pennsylvania or Montana and a trout fisherman from Maine can catch trout in Wyoming just as well if he selects the size of stream he wants. But, invariably, the traveling angler who visits Dan Bailey's country either really wants to know what kind of tackle to bring or wants to hear someone else's opinion, if only to argue about it.

Not many years ago the West was considered a different fishery entirely. When you went West, the story was, you would be on big and violent waters in high winds and be throwing big flies at big trout with big rods. Such fishing was and is available, of course, but there are small meadow streams and tiny spring creeks, the winds don't always blow (not quite, anyway) and not all of the flies or fish are oversize. In fact, from roughly 1970 on there was an increasing interest in delicate fishing out West. It had always been there but the practitioners received less attention than the throwers of big streamers. By 1985 there had been a noticeable slackening in the percentage of late fall distance casters, even though the overall numbers of anglers increased.

We must speak of wading, however, for those who fish the bigger Western rivers need proper equipment for it. Frankly, those who wade regularly along the Yellowstone or Madison in their hurrying sections need not worry about big waters of Canada, Alaska, New Zealand or Argentina. Wading can get only so tough and it does that on the Madison and the Yellowstone. Felt soles serve for most of it but the hard-bitten veterans who want out just a little farther will use some kind of aluminum cleats.

Steelhead or salmon rivers can reach depth and trajectory no one can stand in, but so can the Yellowstone. Anyway, the

Western fisherman equipped for anything that happens will have good chest waders and some kind of soles that will cling to impossible boulders. Wading staffs are gaining popularity.

Now there is likely to be considerable wind in the West, probably more than on most other waters, and the rods and lines reflect it to some extent — but on the smaller streams there are places for a Number Four or Number Five rod, generally around 7½ or 8 feet long in fiberglass, bamboo, graphite or boron. Most of these rods use double taper lines, of course, but there is an occasional caster who prefers a weight forward in deference to considerable wind. The same rods would be at home on the Letort or Battenkill.

But if I took only one rod West it would be a Number Six, probably graphite or boron. That might not be the daintiest for the little creeks but it would do very well there and would handle most of the dry fly and small nymph operations on the big rivers. It works fine from a drift boat but isn't quite enough for the cross-current sinking line operations on wide water. That part of the game is relegated to as powerful a rod as the individual wants to use and Number Ten outfits, at home among steelhead or salt water fish, show up frequently. The big rod isn't needed for fish playing, even for the colorful brown trout spawners of autumn, but it gets distance with big, wind-resistant flies, sometimes weighted, and fast-sinking shooting heads or sinking-tip lines. Of course the big outfits *do* overmatch trout that only occasionally weigh more than three pounds, but there are anglers who have landed their share of big steelhead or tarpon and still like to wade and throw the big lines in a river with brilliant cottonwoods and frost in early morning.

"It's a tour de force!" laughs Ray Donnersberger, who has caught all of those other fish but stands up to his elbows in the Yellowstone in late fall and throws a monstrous nymph on a big rod with a shooting head.

At any rate it's agreed that a Number Seven rod is minimal for slamming two or three inches of streamer across the river.

Trout fishermen follow the policy that one should never carry a single rod if half a dozen will do as well, but there really isn't serious need for more than three. This fact will be ignored but cannot be refuted.

Fly reels work the same everywhere, and the single action is stylish in Montana as well as elsewhere, even though there are some conditions when an automatic would be better. Wading through heavy vegetation in a spring creek, an automatic would save costly fly line that somehow tends to get underfoot and is occasionally partitioned by aluminum cleats.

There are certain dry and wet flies that gained their fame in the West and then graduated to other parts of the country, but

"At any rate it's agreed that a number seven rod is minimal for slamming two or three inches of streamer across the river."

(Red Monical plays a big brown trout hooked on a streamer.)

probably more fly patterns moved West than went the other way. The East was the cradle of American fly fishing and it was the nineteen-thirties before a trip to Montana became anything less than an expedition, whether a fisherman came from New Jersey or California. It was after World War II that the Montana-Yellowstone country really began to produce its own well-known patterns. Still, although there certainly were Rocky Mountain insects that were different, it was still true that a well-supplied fly fisherman from Connecticut or Oregon could catch quite a few fish with what he used at home.

But a supply of flies tailored to the area is better, and on some occasions nothing works as well. A "selection" of flies can range from half a dozen intended for an afternoon on the Madison to a few thousand such as filled the trunk of a tourist's car when I met him on the Gallatin. They were in new plastic boxes and he asked my advice as to which to use, then began to recite the famous tyers who had contributed to his collection. I never saw him use them and am not sure he was willing to get them wet.

Some of the most popular of Western flies have almost disappeared because of line manufacture. Unless he confines all of his operation to conventional dry fly fishing or near-surface streamers, the average angler can gain more by gathering an assortment of fly lines and leaders than by buying more rods and reels. Especially in the West, where water conditions vary from placid pasture creeks to crashing cataracts and their attendant plunge pools, a variety of fly lines, while hardly appealing to the tackle collector, will broaden his efficiency.

In some cases the sinking line in its various forms has made certain flies obsolescent. Heavily weighted nymphs and wet flies with bead eyes lose out under many conditions. The line weight and leader length can be adjusted to put a nymph or streamer at the desired depth. Too much weight in the fly itself sometimes gives less desirable movement than a slow, fast or medium sinking head and a short leader. The line keeps a nymph down and the current gives it natural movement.

On the smaller streams the sinking tip is popular and the high-floating remainder of the line acts as an indicator for gentle takes. Even in the big rivers there is use for sinking tips and when a drift fisherman needs extra depth he may use a "whole" sinking line.

There are some surface film techniques that have come on recently in the more delicate situations. At one time a sinking leader was felt essential to the dry fly's efficiency. Now there are conditions under which the angler actually uses a floating solution for his leader instead of something to make it sink. With tiny terrestrials or emergent nymphs he needs an indicator for a subsurface take and to give him a tight line quickly with a twitch

"If I took only one rod West it would be a Number Six, probably graphite or boron."

of his rod tip — a special kind of fishing. There is a variety of indicators including orange or yellow sleeves for leaders, or bits of yarn. This form of angling has become more popular recently, partly through the added respect for nymphs that gained dignity when separated from ordinary wet flies. And the "soft-hackle" description added to the prestige of the wets. In recent years there has been some return to "casts" of more than one fly although it has never become as popular as it was 50 years ago. Much of Dan Bailey's earlier fishing was with wets, both near Livingston and farther East.

To select some of the most popular flies in our neighborhood it's probably best to take them up by season. The pitfall here is in being too definite as to dates and patterns for any fly mentioned might work at any time. A trout that has been feeding on midges might occasionally feel that a 3-inch sculpin would be good too. For an entire year in all of the local streams and lakes, a list of about 60 flies would cover any situation. That number, which covers both sizes and patterns, was found in the boxes of a regular who fishes all year in Montana. He, of course, was surprised at the number but most anglers would be carrying more. There is one Westerner who claims to fish all year with a single fly in several sizes — dry, wet or on the bottom. Its form is nondescript and its color is black. But more flies work better for most of us and are more fun.

Beginning with winter fishing, a kind seldom done by tourists, the extremes are followed — tiny things during "snow fly" hatches and immense nymphs on the bottom. These are for relatively sluggish fish in most waters and the dead-drifted bottom bumper that imitates a big stone (salmon fly) nymph is productive. Exact imitation of the stone fly nymphs isn't even attempted by most practitioners and the description of "big, soft and dark" almost amounts to a tying formula. Other things take over at other seasons, but some of the nymph lovers insist that they'd catch more than their share of the bigger fish at any time.

In April and May the Stone Fly Nymphs work in both upper and lower Madison and the ubiquitous caddis flies are coming on, sometimes in hatching blizzards. Imitators of the caddis have been less meticulous than those who have copied the thousands of mayflies for centuries.

The caddis was hardly recognized as a basic fly by most Western fishermen until ten years ago, but it now comes very near to being an "all-around" attraction in its various sizes. John Bailey points out that the caddis hatches were mainly handled for better or worse by unrelated artificials like the Wulffs until recently. Nowadays, the big caddis ties pass for grasshoppers sometimes and some of the least ones represent small terrestrials. Considering the number of natural caddis fly forms, there are

Erwin A. Bauer

Erwin Bauer with a Brown trout.

relatively few imitations. The Elk Hair Caddis, a superb floater, is certainly an impression fly with some resemblance to a stunted Muddler Minnow and, effective as it is, it resembles nothing living at close inspection. There are about a dozen caddis patterns popular in Montana but fishermen are likely to simply say, "I used a caddis." When discussing mayflies, they are likely to be more definite. But at least they are beginning to call a caddis a caddis and are less likely to say there were "a lot of those miller-moth things on the water."

June is a high water month in most years and the rivers feel the impact of the past winter's weather that may or may not have left heavy snow packs in the peaks. June is also the stone fly or salmon fly month, and although the giants sometimes hatch on water that is too muddy to fish, the fishing is generally right at some time on some rivers each year, the hatch working upstream and often taking weeks to go from lowest altitude to highest. The Big Hole is generally good by mid-June and stone flies are found on the lower Madison then. In July the hatch has moved well upstream, but is still available. The Yellowstone, usually one of the last to clear, is unreliable for the hatch in the drifting sections but is one of the best if the water is clear enough. Some time after the flies are gone from the Livingston area there may be good salmon fly action in Yellowstone Park.

Although the stone flies have their big inning in June and July, they have their effect the season through. Before and after the mature flies bend the willows and bounce helplessly down the riffles, the giant nymphs are trout staples and imitations of them work for bottom scratching casters. The nymphs are always there. At about the time the stone fly activity grows elsewhere, the Henry's Fork begins its variety of hatches, including the Green Drake, almost as big as the salmon fly. There is little activity on the big salmon fly at famous Railroad Ranch but the nearby Box Canyon should have them by mid-June. Rock Creek should be good by then as well.

Anyone who has fished a productive salmon fly hatch when big fish compete for them is occasionally surprised to find that his flies as well as the naturals drift down unmolested. Timing is difficult to solve but there is a popular theory that fishing is best just as the big naturals begin to fade in a given area. The trout have become used to them and are watching for them.

Drys to imitate the salmon flies need not be close copies, despite a poorly founded theory that the larger the attraction the more carefully it is studied. The Sofa Pillow, evidently originated by Pat Barnes, long-time West Yellowstone tackle store operator and guide and once employed by Bailey's, is simply a buoyant squirrel tail fly, easy to see and approximately the salmon fly colors. And the Muddler Minnow, doped to float, does very well

"... but on the smaller streams there are places for a Number Four or Number Five rod..."

indeed. Neither looks much like a living salmon fly. Perhaps the Elk Hair Salmon Fly is a closer imitation of the real thing. Although it's a bit early for grasshopper season, hopper flies, if big enough, seem to compete pretty well.

Early June is likely to be good dry fly time on big rivers. Big Wulffs, the Trudes, the Goofus and anything else that rides high, floats naturally and is easily visible to trout and angler, does pretty well. The Trude, highly visible with white hair wing, is a true combination, serving as a dry until drag sets in and then doing duty as a streamer. That can be done with a doped Muddler Minnow too. Of late, big caddis flies have gone well and it is a time for dry fly experimentation. Few fishermen use extremely small flies on the Madison or the Yellowstone at this time but Dan Bailey was likely to do it, especially in late evening.

"I catch a lot of whitefish," he grinned, "but I catch a lot of trout too."

He would agree though that the bigger flies — around Number 14 at least, catch more big river fish in most locations. Perhaps we can make exception in the case of the Bighorn — which tends to ruin long-accepted theories. Anyway, late July is likely to be the most productive time of the river year.

August is grasshopper time. Mayflies are not so plentiful. The hoppers have been around all summer but for some reason they get careless in August and tend to take unplanned swimming trips. On windy days the hoppers are especially vulnerable. They aren't studied as are mayfly miniatures but there are some unexplained things about their performances. Any fisherman or cow can kick grasshoppers into the water or scare them in, but there are some days, undistinguished by special weather, when they seem to be especially nautical. Chester Marion, who has done his share of drift fishing in hopper time, especially on the Yellowstone, reports a day when a swarm of hoppers appeared on the water for no discernable reason and brought a charge by hungry trout. Was it an attempted migration to new feeding areas?

Some time in September the dry fly fishing slacks off for most fishermen as far as the bigger streams are concerned although there are specialists who stick with it until snowfall — and catch fish. On the Yellowstone and the Missouri, as elsewhere in big water, the browns are preparing to spawn and take on their bright fall colors to be caught on deep streamers. A few of them could be taken that way all season but pre-spawning pugnacity and need for extra food makes fall the best time.

Some of the most imaginative flies of all are those applied to spawning brown trout, beginning in September and going through most of October on average years. The Muddler Minnow has been altered in dozens of ways, the best known hybrids being the Spuddler, the Marabou Muddler and the white one named the Mizzoulian Spook. In streamers there has been a tendency toward dark colors in deference to the cottus or sculpin but almost all streamer patterns will work. The Spruce Fly in dark and light patterns remains a favorite.

Indian Summer can prolong the late fishing but, usually, somewhere around November 1 the thermometer calls a halt to most action on the bigger rivers. Water is too cold and some of the smaller streams have been slow since early September. Now the big artificial nymphs must move slowly across the bottom and anglers take special interest in spring creeks, the Bighorn and the showoff Fire Hole.

In the big deep-goers for the rivers, the Woolly Buggers have worked well lately, the tie starting out as a Woolly Worm with a tail added. The Girdle Bug or Rubber Leg is a big Woolly Worm with rubber legs added. Getting their start in New Zealand, the Matuka streamers have been popular because they refuse to foul the leader when a cast doesn't go just right.

Bitch Creek Nymphs, again an offshoot of the Woolly Worm, have rubber feelers and tails. Charles Brooks' Montana Stone Fly is another big, dark and soft one. Even some popular salt water patterns have appeared among the late fall streamers.

Although there is a pattern of mayflies becoming scarcer in late summer on most waters, the spring creeks (and the Bighorn) have their own programs. Traditional fly patterns in the smaller sizes work on the spring creeks, of course, and there is more and more interest in emergent flies, some of them of nondescript appearance but effective when trout are taking in the surface film. And there is a trend toward very small flies that carry some sort of signal for a squinting fisherman — a sprig of hair or feather he can see and which will not destroy the illusion for a trout coming up from below. Even some beetles have been tied with a frosted superstructure. The Loop Wing Emerger has a light-colored wing just about to come from the shuck and, incidentally, it is visible to an angler. It mimics nothing likely to hatch, but a very small Royal Wulff often does well among little naturals —and it can be seen.

On barely moving water the Compara-Dun flies have been popular, the bodies riding on the water instead of extended hackles. It is a paradox for fishermen who have sought high-floaters and fingered stiff hackles for many years.

As elsewhere there are the standbys like the Quill Gordon, the Cahills, the Adams and the like that serve regularly when trout are on the surface — except for those frustrating or jubilant days when they are extremely particular and one finds the combination or fails completely. Almost anything works sometimes but when one pattern catches a fish something else might catch a dozen, which is the reason fly fishing is a sport.

II
DAN BAILEY'S WATER

"The Yellowstone below the park is a float river, becoming more and more so through the years."
(Drift boat above Yankee Jim Canyon.)

ONE

The Yellowstone

The Yellowstone River itself has a hold on many other fishermen as it held Dan Bailey. There are business and professional men who are established along the river because of its fishing, following a fly rod with their careers.

And besides the tourist fishermen who fill the motels and guide boats during the season's peak, there is a little-noticed undercurrent of regulars who have built homes along the river, some of them show places, spending most of their summers there. Their pilgrimage is a regular thing and they may spend much of the year's remainder on waters around the world. Others come back to the same motel rooms or efficiencies — people sometimes unnoticed by full-time residents who feel "out-of-staters" are those who spend only a day or two and move on to other mountain scenery. The presence of the regulars contributes more to the economy than shows on the local books.

Many years ago during one of the recurring drives to dam the Yellowstone a famous angler spoke strongly at a mass meeting in Livingston. There were, he said, few streams in the world with the angling appeal of the Yellowstone and any dam would ruin it for the serious fly casters making annual visits.

At that time there was a local leaning toward a dam, regardless of its avowed purpose, for it was thought it would bring water skiers, yachtsmen and other wealthy vacationers — and the verdant ranches of Paradise Valley would be well paid for before they were flooded. The visitor pleading his case said the Yellowstone, undammed, was the attraction that had brought him to the valley every summer for years and a dam would mean the end of his visits.

At that point the "dam lovers" (later, most of them changed

their views, at least temporarily) began to growl ominously and there were scattered boos.

"Go home! We don't need ya here!" some hothead yelled from a center seat — and this outburst brought a brief silence. The crowd suddenly seemed to realize how far their excitement had led them and it was the next day that I made a brief personal summary of the money spent in Livingston by the "outsiders" I knew who spent their summers on "the river." They were, I decided, adjuncts to the community, buying automobiles and other expensive items — and they brought their money with them. They still do. The dam was not built that time as it has not been built on other occasions, but dam builders are persistent and the issue sleeps but does not die.

The Yellowstone is known as a "late" river and the vagaries of sun and snow are puzzling to anglers who hear of fine fishing in February and arrive in July to find the river the color of creamed coffee. The runoff is unpredictable but really not as complex as it seems.

Heavy snowpacks in the mountains generally mean a slow clearup of the river in spring, but as long as the weather is cold enough to prevent a continuous thaw the Yellowstone remains fishable.

"I fish any time the air temperature is more than 55 degrees," Dan Bailey said in his later years, but there had been a time when he fished if the weather reached 40 degrees and occasional trips when the guides froze. Only the years raised his choice of "fishing temperature."

There is the "snow fly hatch" that means midges, which sometimes bring dry fly fishing when skiing and snowmobiling are good. But most of the good winter fly fishing involves big nymphs or Woolly Worms (often nearly the same thing) fished on the bottom with sinking lines and powerful rods. In early spring there may even be hatches of caddis flies that mean fine fishing on top. Traveling fishermen cannot count on these things. Then comes the thaw — or rather the *thaws*. It is hardly fitting to call so large a river a "capsule" of the weather but the Yellowstone demonstrates the program perfectly.

If the snowpack is heavy among the peaks it will generally take a long time to thaw, a process sometimes postponed by brief cool periods. As it thaws it brings the mud down and fly fishermen must turn to small freestone waters or to the reliable spring creeks.

And so there may be several false clearings as temporary chill stops the runoff. Only a practiced eye can come near to a forecast. Heavy snows may fill the valleys and keep the snowplow operators red-eyed but valleys thaw fast, dumping their dirty water into the Yellowstone (or any other river) quickly and then

"Within the park much of the river runs through rough country and fishermen go on foot or horseback into canyon water such as the Seven Mile Hole, where the river is a torrent."
(Ben Williams fishes the Yellowstone's Seven Mile Hole.)

allowing it to clear. The high snows from the Yellowstone Park peaks are less cooperative and there are those years when it is August before the Paradise Valley water is regularly fishable. Even mid-August.

Then there are other problems with runoff. A single tributary river can be the culprit after a "heavy" rain — and that's only a mild rain by the standards of less arid country. The Lamar River, making up in the Park, is bounded by some eroding cliffs and fishermen curse it from a distance of a hundred miles. They stare disconsolately at the soiled Yellowstone and simply say, "It must have rained on the damned Lamar." Then they head for a small creek somewhere or haul their drift boats to the Madison, which can have its own problems although somewhat different from the Yellowstone's.

In the Park, the Yellowstone as it comes out of Yellowstone Lake has cutthroat trout that are sometimes almost too easy to catch but can be a challenge at other times. At Buffalo Ford the anglers sometimes wade almost elbow to reel handle and catch cutthroats that would be individual trophies on much famous water elsewhere.

The cutthroat was the only native trout of Yellowstone country and when rainbows came to Montana and Wyoming from farther West, the brook trout from the East and the brown trout from Europe, they found their ways into the park by a variety of routes. Environmentalists felt the interlopers might destroy the natural ecology of the region, whether they competed directly with cutthroats or not, and the Park Service will not replenish supplies of the invaders — but they prosper along with the cutthroats in many of the park's streams.

Natural barriers have divided the Yellowstone fish precisely. Downstream from Knowles Falls, some distance north of the park boundary (remember, the river is running north) brown trout live along with the rainbows and cutthroats. Then, within the park boundaries, the Yellowstone downstream from Lower Falls holds rainbows as well as cutthroats. Above the falls the population is cutthroat only.

Within the park much of the river runs through rough country and fishermen go on foot or horseback into canyon water such as the Seven Mile Hole, where the river is a torrent. When the cutthroats are on their summer spawning run it may coincide with the hatch of salmon flies and a caster will float big dry imitations close to shore. The standing waves near the river's center are too forbidding for dry flies at that point.

There in such water as Seven Mile Hole are precipitous little tributary creeks, appearing too steep for trout habitation, but the spawning urge carries cutthroats into them and I saw a fisherman, wearing mountain boots instead of waders, kneeling on a boulder

"At Buffalo Ford the anglers sometimes wade almost elbow to reel handle —"

to make a short cast upward, the tiny pool he aimed at being even with his eyes. The cutthroat came for the great Sofa Pillow, a fish too big for its surroundings, and the fisherman gingerly pulled his two-pounder down over a falls.

Downstream to the north the Yellowstone flattens a little after leaving the Park and offers excellent fishing water for all of the local trouts until it crashes into Yankee Jim Canyon, a place where those using drift boats are doing it for adventure rather than relaxation. The fish are there but they are in eddies and pockets along the shore and the river makes itself heard in a tone discouraging to delicate casting.

Yankee Jim once exacted toll from canyon travelers in a long ago time before a trail turned to a road that turned into the smooth asphalt of U.S. 89, going down river to Livingston and up the tributary Shields to Clyde Park, Wilsall, Ringling and White Sulphur Springs.

The Yellowstone below the Park is a float river, becoming more and more so through the years. Before World War II produced a spate of inflatable rubber boats to be used in aircraft rescue and deadly business across enemy streams and along hostile shores, not many floaters used the river. Then when the fishermen came back to the Yellowstone from the wars they brought the surplus rubber rafts and bobbed downstream from one road access to another. The rafts began to look more like real boats and they moved easier with rigid rowing frames. They were not used as the canoe is, being held against the current for steerage instead of outracing it, and they were fine to fish from. They still are. The rafts were refined more and more, became efficient and very expensive and bore trade names instead of government abbreviations and numbers. Then came the johnboats.

Johnboats, like their name, slipped forward from the mists of boating history. They had always been river boats, probably best known in the central and southern United States hill country where a 20-footer could carry a paddling guide and two anglers on canvas chairs for float trips ranging from half a day to half a month. They were square ended with a little turnup at the bow and years later with a heavier transom for outboard motors. For their first 50 years they were mainly wooden but the hill-country folks turned to aluminum and it was the aluminum boat that came to the Yellowstone and the other rivers of the Rockies. The Yellowstone guides and their neighbors fitted them with heavier rowlocks and longer oars and they came down the riffles in comfort, the oarsman holding the boat against the current and stopping it at good wading locations. There still are johnboats. Then came the McKenzie.

The "McKenzie" boat is nearly a duplicate of the salt water

". . . it was the aluminum boat (johnboat) that came to the Yellowstone and other rivers of the Rockies."
(Guide Ray Hurley lining johnboat through Yellowstone side channel.)

"Then when the fishermen came back to the Yellowstone from the wars they brought the rubber surplus rafts and bobbed downstream from one road access to another."
(Merton Parks watches a client fish - about 1960.)

dory that has carried codfishermen and their ilk for hundreds of years and were nested on the decks of deep water sailing ships and then steamships — ships from much of Europe that brought Portugese words to Canadian Indians before Columbus confused his navigation. Then the McKenzie was used on wild rivers on many locations in the United States and Canada. Its high sides and wave scaling efficiency were not really necessary on rivers like the Yellowstone and Madison but it was comfortable and impressed a guide's clients. It worked fine and became a status symbol. People who had hardly ever fished before its coming ran the rivers regularly and their trailered drift boats decorated their yards.

Manufacturers didn't use the name, "McKenzie," much and perhaps it will some day become something like "johnboat," a word neither descriptive nor traceable. Anyway, it may be the ultimate drift boat, superseding the dugout canoe and all of the other craft that came after it.

When the Yellowstone clears early the stonefly hatch is the big news. It begins far down the rivers, moving upstream with predictable regularity, and if the river is clear in June the huge flies will be flailing awkwardly about on the part of the river best known to visiting anglers. The giant stonefly nymphs might be a good lure at other times of year but when the hatch is under way most fly fishermen use big drys. At that time bigger fish that would usually be concentrating on things like sculpins down near the bottom find bumbling two-inch insects worthy of their attention.

Cast one of dozens of stonefly imitations or other flies of similar size against the stone banks and where water boils around willows. It is no time for delicacy and hair tippets for the strikes are likely to be loud glugs and the fish's size unpredictable. It is no time for tiddlers.

Many traveling fishermen hope to make their trip at "salmon fly" time but it is unpredictable, especially on the Yellowstone, and after a long trip they are likely to find the river brown instead of blue-green. Don't count on it. The Madison is more reliable, is regulated by dams and clears earlier anyway.

Before and after the salmon fly hatch there is good fishing with big, highly visible dry flies and the Trude may be used as much on the Yellowstone as anywhere else, a fly that imitates everything and nothing, carrying a white hair wing that works well under water too, when it becomes a streamer. It's highly visible to the fisherman and when it drags he can simply hurry his retrieve and pretend he was streamer fishing in the first place. Muddler Minnows can be fished wet or dry and it has been said that small white Muddler is the world's most reliable trout fly. Anyway, summer dry fly fishing on the Yellowstone means

"The *McKenzie Boat* is nearly a duplicate of the salt water dory —" (Ray Hurley launches his drift boat on the Yellowstone.)

big, showy things that bounce along in the riffle "corners" and glide pertly near the centers of dozens of side channels. Then, in late summer comes grasshopper time.

There are a number of grasshopper patterns with names and more that have not gained that distinction. They are fished much as the salmon fly is, cast close to the shoreline and dead-drifted —but since a seagoing live grasshopper is likely to show energetic concern over his impromptu venture, an artificial may be taken when moved by a sloppy leader. Then, as the cooling days shorten, comes streamer time. It generally begins in September when the aspens on the high slopes change from light green splotches against darker conifers to gaudy yellow. The cottonwoods are changing too and the wild rosebushes have been reddish for some time.

There were other casters who threw long lines and big flies into cold Yellowstone water at about the same time, or even earlier, but Joe Brooks, the fishing writer, popularized the streamer fishing. Certainly Dan Bailey did it and enjoyed it but it was not really his favorite method.

Brooks and his cohorts brought bigger rods to the river — rods that were built for bass bug fishing or even heavier operations, and they double-hauled their weight-forward lines far out into the heavy currents of the big pools. Double haul? This was the Fifties and Dan Bailey had never needed it before. The distance casting came almost directly from the tournament masters by way of West Coast steelhead rivers, and after Dan Bailey had mastered the technique and used it occasionally, he agreed that it caught bigger fish than anything else he had tried. But at one of Helen Bailey's dinner parties he talked long and earnestly with Wes Jordan, rod designer, exhibition caster and internationally known member of the Orvis staff.

Dan turned apologetically to his other guests.

"Wes and I were just talking about fishing on small creeks," Dan said. "We both began that way."

Once the long cast, big fly, big fish approach got its start, it moved rapidly. The big fish, they said, were near the bottom and even a heavy-hooked Muddler with no dressing didn't get down that far on a floating line. So the more ardent ones went to the sinking shooting head with monofilament backing. At first, Joe Brooks said it wasn't really fly fishing, even though it grew from his long-cast, mid-river technique — but he finally accepted it.

Now we were really steelheading our trout river, down to a short leader to keep the streamer or giant nymph inches from the bottom — and although Theodore Gordon, the Adirondack recluse of another century, would have wondered what was going on, the long casters waded deeper and threw farther. It was different but it had its own special appeal on the Yellowstone as on other Western rivers that roared instead of muttering.

It works best after the first snows show on the Absoraka peaks. If the snow has fallen in Paradise Valley it has melted quickly but the cattle are being brought down from the high pastures at a time when ranchers look like ranchers in chaps and broad hats and their horses strut a little as if to say that this is what they were meant for all along. Sometimes the highways are temporarily blocked by waves of beef and tourist kids press their noses against car windows to see "real cowboys." At other times the cowboys might ride hay balers and wear baseball caps and even tennis shoes, but for the time being they fit their heritage, and the tourist kids are right.

It is a special time. The big streamers usually work best in late afternoon when the mountain shadows stalk a fisherman who is above his waist in heavy water, feeling the gravel work a little under his aluminum cleats. It is spawning time for brown trout, the males villainous with their hooked jaws but gaudy in spawning colors and the females beautifully colored too. It is hard to believe that American anglers of 100 years ago cursed the newly arrived brown trout and said its appearance was inferior.

The sinking head is thrown far across heavy currents, usually a little upstream, the big streamer sinking slowly with the current until it is caught by the wild swing of the bellying line —and although the fish might take during that brief period it may follow the hurrying stranger all the way across and strike when the fly is almost stationary again as it stops its swing almost directly below the caster. The fisherman has retrieved his shooting line, probably a limp monofilament, most of the coils dropping in the water and probably at least two of them held in his mouth. He can cast farther in fast water if he uses monofilament for it sinks near his feet when there is nothing to hold it near the surface — and when he casts it holds back the shooting head. Perhaps he uses lightweight shooting line that floats and picks up easier but is not quite so smooth through the guides and he speaks endlessly on the subject with other fall fishermen.

There are big rainbows too sometimes but it is the brown trout that usually come in the largest fall sizes and a large share of the Bailey wallfish are fall dated. The fall "run" continues into November but very few visiting fishermen are around at its end and most of the residents are following game trails or bird dogs. The fall crusade is less popular in recent years, a matter of increasing interest in entomology and Latin names. The "technical" trout fishermen are the new heroes.

But it is a special time when the big streamers and frightening imitation nymphs sweep down the current, swiftly at the pool's head, a little more slowly in the waist and still slower in the pool's broadened tail where brown trout are surveying for bedding areas.

The late October fisherman is likely to be alone, feeling a chill that searches for gaps in his down, wool and rubber armor, and he can hear the distant boom of a deer hunter's rifle somewhere above the bench. A flight of mallards hisses past, heads twisting at the unfamiliar obstacle in the big pool, and when he wades stiffly ashore at dusk he ears the musical conversation of geese searching for their gaps in mountains to the south. In a few days there will be slush ice whispering its way downstream, the cottonwoods and aspen are almost bare and there are snow clouds up Paradise Valley.

"But most of the good winter fly fishing involves big nymphs or Woolly Worms (often nearly the same thing) fished on the bottom with sinking lines and powerful rods."
(Don Williams, Yellowstone guide, fishes the river during a snowstorm.)

Lewistown Spring Creek

TWO

Spring Creeks

Dan said Armstrong's Spring Creek was wonderful but that it had one grievous fault.

"A Number 16 Light Cahill is it," Dan said. "The fish aren't easy to catch but all you need is one fly. There should be a little variety."

There was the long ago time when we seldom used but the one fly on the spring creeks and we catered to a bankers' hours hatch between 10 a.m. and 2 p.m. After years of that, I was leaving Armstrong's one day, the hatch concluded, when I saw an infidel from Oklahoma wade into the creek and begin catching fish on a nymph. As anglers became more learned and began to stay all day we sagely announced that the creeks had changed and that the hatches were more varied.

Perhaps there has been some such change but for the most part it is probably the fishermen rather than the fish who have altered their ways. In those old days few ever planned to spend a full day on Nelson's or Armstrong's Spring Creek. As Red Monical said, you'd simply go to the creek during the hatch and at 2 o'clock you'd head for the Yellowstone. On one such occasion I fished Armstrong's until "quitting time," and then worked the Yellowstone until dusk. Then as I crossed Armstrong's on the way back to the car, I idly slapped a big Muddler into a gently gurgling run and you have guessed what happened. It seemed some sort of sacrilege and I kept quiet about it.

I recall going to Armstrong's at around 9:15 one morning and was staring at the gliding water with its undulating submerged plants, knowing I was too early. There was nothing to break the surface — not even a brash tiddler chasing an errant terrestrial. Two traveling fishermen arrived and began rigging their rods. They didn't lower their voices much.

"Do you suppose that's old Joe picking out a spot?" one of them said, nodding toward me. I was flattered to be taken for Joe Brooks, who had done so much to make the creek famous. I tried to be helpful. I went over to the newcomers and told them that the hatch and subsequent rise would start in about 30 minutes. They stared arrogantly at this red-necked prophet and then grinned at each other before turning their backs on me.

Then they walked into the creek's center and started wading rapidly upstream, slapping flies along the shore as they went. They walked as close together as they could without interfering with each other's casting and they splashed a great deal in the shallow parts. They went for approximately 300 yards about as fast as they could walk on uneven bottom and among islands of vegetation. Then they got out of the creek, laughed loudly and said so much for the great spring creek.

"We had one damned strike," they announced as they returned to the gate where I was waiting, implying that the creek and I were of the same caliber. They were taking off their waders when the first mayflies fluttered on the surface and the first of the rises bloomed silently in the slick runs.

I started into the water and had the gall to point out that the trout were now beginning to work, but they turned their backs on me and climbed into their car. They had come a long way to prove that this delicate spring creek business was baloney and they weren't about to be dissuaded.

The creeks became attractions for anglers who were so awed by spring creek accounts that they lacked the confidence to fish there themselves. Stumbling through one of the swifter sections below the crossover I somehow hooked a 10-inch brown trout one morning after a hundred fruitless casts and was astounded to hear polite applause from the bank. There stood two men and two ladies and I have no idea how long they had been there for my concentration had blacked out most of the world.

"We sure enjoyed that," said one of the men while the others grinned broadly. "We wouldn't think of trying it ourselves but we drove 200 miles just to see the place."

They turned toward their car and whatever I said probably sounded idiotic for it was one of few times I have been mistaken for a spring creek expert.

Spring creek fishing has at times been treated with a gravity hard to comprehend for non-anglers. In more recent years the abilities of technical fishermen have increased enormously and the day has gone when the mere efficient casting of a Number 18 fly was considered remarkable. I ruefully remember the perfectionist who arrived with handmade cane rods with hand-fitted grips. His flies could best be appreciated with a magnifying glass and I learned a great deal from him. We had him and his wife

Angler with a standby rubber boat fishes a spring creek near Livingston.

Bill Browning Photo

to dinner and we went fishing on Armstrong's. It was tough that day.

He'd caught a fish or two before he chose a deep glide to be reached with a fairly long cast and began to work over what seemed to be a single rising fish. It was a little late in the day and the main hatch was over. I went upstream in search of the occasional simple-minded trout to be found even at Armstrong's. I found none and came back. Our expert was still applying flies to the slick and the fish was still working occasionally.

"I guess I'll give up," he said, shaking his head. "This one is too much for me."

To furnish a little comic relief I sloshed into the spot where he had been standing, worked out a little line and slopped a Number 18 Light Cahill on roughly the place where the trout had been showing. From somewhere, a salmonid idiot tore across the surface and took my fly with a coarse sound. I landed it and was surprised to see that it looked like any other trout despite its obvious feeble-mindedness.

"See," I joked as I released it. "All it takes is skill and science."

There was no answer and when I looked up our new friends were striding toward their car in silence. We never saw them again. Trout fishing can be serious business. I kept a couple of beautiful flies those folks gave us and I wish they would come back. They were really good.

The boom in "technical" fishing came in recent years. Those who have eagerly placed their names on a reservation list for a paid rod on one of the spring creeks are surprised to learn that there was a time when there was no charge to fish and generally no fishermen at all. I cannot say how the fishing then compared to what it is now but I'd guess the catches were less consistent. I think there were more big fish and fewer small ones but there is no record. I do recall one Labor Day when Armstrong's gave up a number of fine fish, several of which were around three pounds — an unusual size today. But there weren't very many fish caught that time — just a few big ones.

The Armstrong creek flows through the property of Allyn O'Hair and then through that of the Warren DePuy estate. Both charge rod fees for fishing it. Water rights, nearly always vague, are especially so when a stream is very close to a large river like the Yellowstone, where river bed and high water lines are in a constant state of flux. The Armstrong Spring Creek name comes from Paul Armstrong, Mrs. O'Hair's father. Most anglers simply call the lower part "DePuys."

Until twenty-some years ago, all of the Armstrong stream was regulated by the Armstrong-O'Hair people and the DePuy Creek was separate. Then Warren DePuy built a dam that diverted all of the Armstrong Creek to his property, where it joined his original

"Much of Armstrong spring Creek comes from a big spring at the original Armstrong homesite—"

creek. When the DePuy dam was built there was a lawsuit to prevent the diversion, with Paul Armstrong instituting the action, but the dam remained, forming a small lake while shortening the O'Hair and Armstrong section. Dan Bailey worked hard in behalf of the Armstrong interests, feeling that the stream would be better fishing if left to its original course.

Much of Armstrong Spring Creek water comes from a big spring at the original Armstrong homesite, the rest of it rising less dramatically farther up the valley.

On the other side of the Yellowstone is the famous Nelson Spring Creek, also paid fishing, and operated by Mr. and Mrs. Edwin Nelson. The lower part of it, owned by other interests, is not open to public fishing. Both Armstrong and Nelson creeks have waiting lists during the warmer months.

Until 1970 the Armstrong creek had been open to all fishermen but popularity of such waters made it desirable to either lease it or charge rod fees by the day. Dan Bailey was instrumental in a Trout Unlimited project for leasing. Contributors made up a fund that secured the creek for a limited number of anglers through reservations. When the lease ran out it seemed too difficult to raise money for another and the O'Hairs began their daily fee program.

Paid fishing on such creeks becomes a necessity if they are to be maintained as quality water and made accessible to the public. The other alternative, and one Dan Bailey hoped would not occur, would be private leases for persons who could afford personal fishing of high quality. Dan wanted such waters to be open to as many anglers as they could accommodate, even if they had to pay.

Spring creek anglers are serious operators. Now and then an unorthodox method attracts attention or is misunderstood. My wife, a bit too small for deep wading, found that there were some especially large trout living in a slough off the Armstrong creek and employed a floater bubble to get at them. On one day, after she had fought several of the big ones from her tiny craft in the weed-choked backwater, a kindly angler walked over from the creek.

"You can't catch those fish in there, lady," he said. "To catch fish you have to go over to the creek where the water runs."

Since the spring creek temeratures don't fluctuate the way those of freestone streams do, late fall fishing can be good, long after most tourist fishermen have gone home. There is a special appeal to rising trout when the banks are snow-covered and flights of geese are high and headed for mountain passes. On some days the creek's steam freezes in gleaming ice on the bare cottonwoods and the stream's course must look like a white highway to ducks fresh from Canada.

"You can't catch those fish in there, Lady," he said. "To catch fish you have to go over to the creek where the water runs."

Many years ago I used to hunt ducks on Armstrong's, and one Thanksgiving Day I carried a shotgun toward the creek through a light snowfall to see a single fisherman changing flies in midstream. It was the late Merton Parks, the dry fly master of Gardiner, Montana, who made his home there because the trout live in such places as Armstrong's and the Yellowstone. He watched the fading circle of a trout's rise below a swatch of broken water.

"This is the best time of all," he said.

The spring creeks are wreathed in sentiment and nostalgia. I once wrote a flowery comment on them and quote it from a book long out of print:

"And as the fish come to the spring creek through preference, most of them descendants of those that have turned from the broad river, so do the fishermen come to such a shrine, speaking eagerly to those of their kind, having less to say to cruder fishermen.

"They park their expensive cars and battered pickup trucks at the weathered wooden gate and dismount in their faded jeans and English tweeds, and stand for a moment to watch the placid surface for the beginning of a hatch. They are very different people, even yet, but then they struggle into waders and vests and slip their felted feet gently into the stream, and somehow they all look very much alike."

"—but then they struggle into waders and vests and slip their felted feet gently into the stream, and somehow they all look very much alike."

"Dan's favorite spot on Sweetgrass featured meadow beaver ponds."

THREE

Sweetgrass

Dan kept talking about Sweetgrass Creek and said it was his kind of trout stream, although I don't know of any trout streams that weren't Dan's kind. Anyway, Sweetgrass comes out of the Crazy Mountains and feels its way through the foothills and ranches down toward the Yellowstone. It is not one of the famous streams and I am not trying to send you there for you probably wouldn't find the good places anyway.

But like the Shields River on the other side of them, Sweetgrass Creek has special attraction because it comes out of the Crazies. The Crazy Mountains gouge upward out of comparatively level land and they are high enough to carry little snow patches when the surrounding ranchland shimmers a little in summer heat. Like most mountains, the Crazies take up much more space than they appear to at first, but it is not only the truly high peaks that awe me. Also, it is the expanses of cow country and crops at their feet.

Long before you reach the actual thrust of the jutting mountains themselves, you think it will be just a little farther. You cross thousands of acres of grassland, sage and grainfields, surprised to find that there is still another ranch between you and the truly steep part — and yet another.

Spike Van Cleve, author of intriguing books about his life as a rancher and dude rancher below the Crazies, wrote of his town of Melville, now hardly noticeable except for its church, and told of a life on thousands of acres the casual highway traveler would not even notice as they are foreshortened between the road and the peaks. Melville, not far from Big Timber, was still a frontier town of sorts when the word "frontier" lived mainly in Western history.

It's hard to leave the Crazy Mountain subject and it is hard to think of nearby communities except in conjunction with the peaks. I think of Clyde Park and Wilsall to the west as being "beneath" the Crazies although most of their residents probably don't feel that way at all. Still, they pass on some of the Crazy Mountain stories, like the one of stolen gold cached somewhere in them by a fleeing and mortally wounded gunman. And they have some of their personal stories of screaming Crazy mountain winds and searing electrical storms leaping about the high cliffs.

Not many years ago there were the two local ranchers, exploring in the peaks, who met one of the great roaring lightning storms and shook hands among the crackling charges on the boulders, feeling only one might get out to tell the story. They both made it but they spoke softly of it.

Access to the national forest land of the Crazies is not easy, but for some years we hunted deer and blue grouse up there, and when in the Crazies with Ben Williams I returned the bugling of a proddy bull elk and was a little dismayed to find him and his retinue of cows almost in my lap. We told him in plain English to leave. We carried grouse guns.

Ben and John Bailey and I climbed into the Crazies to fish in Swamp Lake — no great hiking expedition, except that we chose to spend the night when the wind was blowing, and I suspect it nearly always does. As we neared the lake, set high among the peaks, we found junipers distorted into ground-hugging caricatures of trees. It was difficult to pitch our backpacking tents and the wind would die somewhat, only to return from the distance with a sound like a flight of jet fighters. That is not an exaggeration. I do not know what speeds it attained but when John lost his hat it disappeared in the sky, roughly toward Billings, at unbelievable speed. Ben stood on a boulder the next morning, trying to get his fly into the water but the wind blew him off into shoreline shallows — and that was only a breeze compared to what we'd had the night before.

When I first saw the Crazies and thought I was at their very feet I asked a resident how far it was to where I could observe some of the mountain goats, then quite plentiful there. He said it would be seven miles by truck and then, he said, we could start hiking into the mountains. The whole thing is on a grand scale. Strangely, when there is an early snowstorm the Livingston residents stand beneath their monumental Absorakas and inquire, "Did you see the Crazies this morning?"

Dan's favorite spot on the Sweetgrass featured meadow beaver ponds. He marked the map I have before me, telling where to request permission, for the ponds are on private land. When we finally got there I thought again that I was at the foot of the mountains but Andy Dana, who had worked for a dude ranch farther upstream, said the fish were bigger there.

We found Dan's beaver ponds (I somehow think of them as belonging to Dan instead of to the rancher) and went to work with dry flies. There were small brook trout, even in the badly silted-in pools, and it was a while before we caught bigger ones. The ponds were not formed from Sweetgrass itself but from a seepy tributary creek to one side.

In one little stretch, long remembered later because of a jagged tree stump along the ridge, the creek was quite deep at center, going darkly through a pattern of emergent vegetation and a boggy edge. I had put my big dry fly in the center of the deep channel and watched it disconsolately as it moved downstream very slowly. Then I twitched it and a very good brook trout grabbed it — so we continued fishing that stretch with twitched dry flies and caught a dozen brook trout.

As we finished the day we walked past a very old beaver pond that through some vagary of current had retained depth, even though the beaver dams had evidently been largely replaced by new earth lodged in their rotting structure (beavers build valley floors through centuries of dams that catch mountain silt). In this case there was actually a little clump of trees that had taken years to grow. I got the fly into the water past some low-hanging branches and a good brown trout came with a rush from a tangle of submerged brush. Two pounds? I released him with smug satisfaction.

A month later I came that way with my wife Debie and Harry Murray, the Virginia angling master. Debie was fishing around a bend.

"Right over there by that brush," I said to Harry, "I caught a brown trout that would weigh something like two pounds."

With that I somehow duplicated the cast that had taken the brown trout earlier and he came again with an urgent rush and took the fly with a plop.

"Hey, Debie!" called Harry irreverently. "He caught old Dum Dum again!"

I do not know if there was anything personal between Dan Bailey and that trout, but I thought I could make out Dan's boot tracks on the bank I cast from.

"There are both more fish and more fishermen on Rock Creek than there were when we first fished there with Dan Bailey...."

FOUR

Rock Creek

There are both more fish and more fishermen on Rock Creek than there were when we first fished there with Dan Bailey, results of more careful management and added restrictions.

Let's say there are 50 miles of Rock Creek, a tributary of the Clark Fork, and most of it is easily followed if a fisherman doesn't mind a slightly rough gravel road. The Rock Creek Road leaves Interstate 90 only 20 miles east of Missoula, which has some 34,000 inhabitants and is a western version of a true city. Missoula spreads wide.

I've caught a lot of fish on Rock Creek, but in those days I don't recall taking anything very large. Down in the Clark Fork we've caught some much bigger fish, using big streamers in fall.

I can remember camping next to a monumental beaver project on Rock Creek and spending a large part of a morning watching the dam makers at work, but there was very little beaver dam fishing on those early trips. Anyway, it was a pleasant place and someone organized a true camping expedition. There were six of us, including Joe and Mary Brooks, who strongly favored Rock Creek, and Dan and Helen Bailey.

I can't recall much about the equipment except that the Baileys had an umbrella tent which required a little thought for setting up. Helen directed the procedure and Dan moved about inside the shapeless heap of canvas, a head-shaped knob here and there. Dan complained that such construction took up valuable fishing time.

Not everything went smoothly on that trip. Fishing was pretty good but Debie, who was experimenting with aluminum foil cooking, didn't get the buried potatoes quite done and was somewhat crestfallen. Helen fell into Rock Creek while wading and was short of dry clothes. We lost Dan.

When we got up the first morning the women folk were doing their best with a super breakfast. Dan liked super breakfasts but was more interested in fishing and began to don his waders before the hotcakes were done. Someone had left a bucket of cold water standing near the fire and while Dan, the master wader with a gymnast's sense of balance, was putting on his waders he hopped around and stepped backward into the bucket of near-ice water with his dry foot.

"Look," said Dan. "I stepped into the bucket."

This mild report was a typical Bailey reaction to such things and its humor has grown with the years. He wrung out his sock, laughed at himself and ate some hotcakes. He nearly burned his fly line.

His mind set on the upcoming fishing, Dan started to dress his fly line, a business that may not have been absolutely necessary with the modern kinds — but Dan, like the rest of us, remembered the days of silk lines and the necessity for constant care. He fastened his leader end to a tree and looked for another tree just the right distance for keeping the line off the ground while he dressed it. This took some time since the rest of us were milling around the place with the women cooking and Brooks and I offering advice. Dan would carefully lift his line over people's heads as he sought the perfect tree. For a moment I concentrated on the cooking and stiffened with Dan's mild remark:

"Look," he said with what was very nearly a giggle, "I stretched my line right over the fire!" And then Dan Bailey moved very fast indeed, after which he told everyone how stupid he had been. That evening we lost Dan.

Fishing was pretty slow. Now at that time Joe and Dan, always very close friends, had a mutual problem: Both had suffered heart ailments and had been warned about excessively strenuous activities. Brooks, ex-heavyweight boxer, baseball pitcher (he'd had a big-league chance if he'd wanted it) and top-notch golfer, was a little worried about Dan.

"You and I are a couple of spooks," Dan had told him, meaning neither of them would have been on the streams before advanced medical developments. Of course Dan didn't show up at dinner time.

When it began to get dark, Joe insisted on a search.

"Dan is in no condition to be running around this long on that creek," Joe said.

He and I began driving up and down the Rock Creek road and inquiring of everyone we met. The word was out that a fast-walking man in waders and with a fly rod had disappeared. There were a number of camps along the creek and we stopped at each one.

"This is now a job for the sheriff's force," Joe said. "Let's get to a telephone."

A few minutes after that, Dan appeared in the headlights beside the road. He was tinkering with his fly box.

"The fish didn't really start rising until after dark," Dan said. "I believe this fly needs a little more hackle — "

Both Brooks and Bailey lived for many years after that.

Dan Bailey checks the waders while Joe Brooks looks on. Debie Waterman is working at the cook table. Camp is on Rock Creek.

Erwin A. Bauer fishes Madison River in Yellowstone National Park.

FIVE

Madison River

We had a typewritten page of people and places to contact in Montana and Dan Bailey was at the top of the list along with the Yellowstone River, but the Yellowstone was muddy. It was around the first of July. Our list had been typed by Joe Brooks.

Dan told us to go to Ennis and try the Madison. We didn't buy much at Bailey's store, which, I'm afraid, hadn't been properly underlined on the Brooks list. He'd taken it for granted we knew all about Bailey's but we didn't, and for that matter the Madison was just another name to us — a famous name, we knew, but in 1957 I'd been just a little vague as to what Western state it ran through.

Since Livingston wasn't in very large letters on the road map we'd concluded the place to get equipment on the way West would be in Denver, so that's where we stopped and got a few things, including some new stockingfoot waders for me. Then, on to Montana. Bailey's shop had more stuff than the place we'd visited in Denver and maybe I should have asked Dan about waders — but more on that.

In those days it wasn't hard to rent an apartment in Livingston. For years we simply drove into town and checked a newspaper for apartments to rent and we always had one before dark. In fact, we generally had time to fish a little before moving in if we felt like it. The price was right and later real estate page students might like to know that an efficiency apartment ran somewhere around $40 a month. At Joe Brooks' recommendation we'd already decided to headquarter in Livingston. The first year's apartment was upstairs and the folks who rented it to us were a little older than we were. The man was interested in angling wanderers and it developed he had driven stagecoach teams that hauled tourists in Yellowstone Park.

"I once lost a good horse coming down that mountain," he mused. I'm sorry I can't remember what mountain it was. It would mean more today. And now we are the old timers.

Then we went to Ennis and moved into a motel, the Riverside, then owned by Bud and Mike (Mary Ann) Baker. We wandered upstream from Ennis and waded into what looked like good water. The bottom was slippery but I tried my revolutionary new wading gear. I'd applied some carborundum chips to the shoes with the recommended stickum and found I had the footing of a mountain goat. So when I saw what looked like better water on the other side, I simply walked across the wide, swift and shallow Madison. No problem.

For almost two hours I fished around the far side of the river with mediocre success, then decided to go back to the old Oldsmobile on the road side. But the metal chips had worn off my shoe soles and I ended up by actually swimming most of the way, figuring it was safer to swim than to stumble and fall. Debie decided it was very funny that I was drenched and I sportingly joined in the laughter. It was three days later that I remembered the Leica I had been carrying in my vest. The repairman did his best, then advised I trade it in on something.

We struck the salmon fly hatch just right a little below the Varney bridge. In the section we worked it was not quite typical and for some reason the fish were mainly in midriver rather than along the edges. It is Madison water, and early in July the rounded rocks are likely to be greasy-slick with growth.

We began with big dry flies and the Sofa Pillow seemed as good as any. I do not know how many two and 3-pound brown trout we caught but through several days we weighed them carefully with Bailey's 4-pound Wall-of-Fame in mind. We never made it but we came close several times — and it was there that my wife learned to throw a long fly line. The fact that the big browns were out near the middle and that Debie couldn't wade very far into the Madison and remain upright changed her tactics. Up to that time she hadn't bothered with things like the double haul. I had landed only a few of the bigger ones when I noticed her Sofa Pillow was out there with mine and the trout liked it just as well.

She felt that our Sofa Pillows weren't quite big enough and felt that a fish faced by thousands of 2-inch salmon flies might want something bigger for dessert. In Baker's motel she announced she would tie a Sofa Pillow that would never sink, even in the boiling Madison currents, and that any perceptive trout would recognize it as something better than ordinary.

Now the original Sofa Pillow evidently got its start with Pat Barnes, long-time Montana angler and guide, who operated a shop and guide service in West Yellowstone. The name came when a client looked at the big fluffy squirrel hair creation and said it was a "regular sofa pillow," according to Pat.

"We struck the salmon fly hatch just right a little below the Varney Bridge." (Wading the Madison in 1957.)

Debie used a big, long hook and tied on more and more hackle until the thing seemed to have little contact with the water, bobbing drily down the plunging Madison to put the real salmon flies to shame. It did not look like a salmon fly but it was a sort of super something that the trout glugged with enthusiasm. I named it the "Haystack Fly," and wrote a feature about it for Outdoor Life. At the time, not being versed in fly nomenclature, I did not know there was another Haystack Fly somewhere else. Those who accepted ours saved me by calling it the "Madison Haystack." Names for new flies are getting as hard to produce as names for registered bird dogs.

We fished the hatch for several days and then turned mainly to big Muddler Minnows when the salmon flies had carried their hatch far upstream into the Park. The Muddlers were easy to handle. We'd let them float as far as they were willing to, and then let them swing under and around. More good browns, one of which went three pounds and 15 ounces. We camped by the river on several occasions that year and there were no drift boats and hardly any other fishermen. On our last visit that fall I chiseled my initial on a rock beside the river, through a lifetime my only venture into graffiti.

There is a great deal of the Madison, best known for its rush down the valley, but in some higher places it is "technical" water with placid pools where a dimpled rise shows plainly, and in others, like the Bear Trap Canyon, it crashes and boils over boulders in standing waves that no one cares to wade. Between are the lakes and their unique fisheries, and finally the Madison levels out again, gathering its tributaries into the confluence with the Jefferson and Gallatin. Then it is the Missouri.

Drift boats have crowded sections of the Madison because it is likely to be fishable in early season when similar-sized rivers are muddy. All along the river fishing pressure has been relieved by sectional regulations covering catch-and-release water and prohibiting drift fishing altogether in some stretches. There is such a variety of fishing on the Madison that tourist anglers have difficulty discussing their experiences. It often sounds as if the other fellow has been fishing somewhere else entirely.

In Yellowstone Park it's been said the river runs through a zoo since fishermen are likely to be in close contact with elk and buffalo. Most water there is easily reached from a highway. Below the Park the river runs into Hebgen Lake and Quake Lake.

"Gulper" fishing got its name at Hebgen Lake as far as I know, and it's a matter of good trout feeding steadily on very tiny flies, usually at dawn and dusk. Some of the fishermen wade but almost any kind of a boat is a help. My first gulper experience was with Gene Decker and we got out there early on a very chilly morning. I saw that the gulper aficionado is a special breed, tying unique flies and plotting continually, the reason being that no one has really solved the problems that go with gulpers. We were going to fish from shore and Gene looked determined as we slipped into the water. There was steam rising here and there and already there were boats slipping about on what was very nearly a flat calm at dawn.

Since I knew the flies were tiny and the fishing technical, I was equipped with my current pride and joy, a bamboo rod that was too short and too light for what was about to happen. I couldn't reach out far enough. Gene had more rod and before long he caught a pretty good fish in an area where boat anglers hadn't seemed to be scoring. Since the steadily gulping trout were obviously eating an almost microscopic spinner that coated the surface by the thousands, I was a little surprised to see that Gene's effective fly was a shapeless thing that looked more like a wad of lint than anything else. He explained.

"These fish," Gene said, "are taking these things that are so small they're trying to get several flies at one slurp. So this fly of mine represents a whole wad of these things that have been clumped together by wind."

He let me use one and I finally hooked a good fish that had wandered too near shore where the ground was boggy. I lost the fish but did not drown, making the morning a partial success. I have forgotten the name of Gene's fly, and by this time he may have too. Using the term "pattern" in connection with an irregular collection of feather or hair scraps is not apropos.

I believe it was in this area that my friend put forth with his floater bubble (belly boat) and as he paddled his way out over 10 feet of water and began to work out his fly line he noted the occupants of a nearby boat were eyeing him with disfavor. In fact, they informed him that they were in the cove first and that he was an impolite interloper. My friend, a bit broad in the shoulder anyway, rose to the occasion with a paragraph like those I think of too late.

"There's room on this lake for all of us," he said firmly, "and, incidentally, I'm not floating in this thing. I'm standing on the bottom."

The Madison has very large trout, a great many of them, and some of the regulars have learned to probe the bottom with big flies, not only during early and late seasons, but even when dry flies are working. Charles E. Brooks, who has written some of the most enlightening trout books concerning the area, has been a specialist on the bottom bumpers. The huge nymph patterns have most frequently represented the giant stone fly nymph but very different things have worked well too. The big trout are simply used to big things and have happily accepted all sorts of apparitions with fuzzy bodies and rubber legs.

I once fished some Madison water with George Anderson, the

tackle man and guide, who is especially proficient with bottom bouncing. George, like most Montana anglers, is willing to wade in water that slants and bellows, and he chose a section near Slide Inn where the boulders are as large as Chryslers, the river narrow and steep. There wasn't much of a hatch and I'd come to see how George fished a nymph on the bottom anyway. His system was to attach a split shot sinker well above a nymph, and fish it on a short and fairly taut line with a colorful leader and a little sleeve of orange marker. His success was phenomenal and even I caught a trout or two that way as well as more whitefish than I really wanted to see. The small pockets and plunging currents are perfect for Anderson's approach with the short line. As the light faded on my trip with George, I noted that a number of dry fly anglers had simply stopped and watched the water.

The varied fishing of the Madison has led to varied philosophies and my ears burn a little when I think of the day I spent with big Muddlers on a rod I also used for salt water. I had done very well and had closely approached my current goal, which was to get a 4-pound fish for Bailey's Wall Of Fame.

"Flushed with success," as they used to say about a winning army, I paused in roaring midstream to see a mature fisherman going cautiously along next to shore, laying a small dry fly daintily beside a series of swirls caused by underwater boulders. I felt kindly toward the world of lesser anglers and I sloshed toward him to inquire how fishing had been. There was little he could do except ask me the same question and I proclaimed my achievements as if giving box scores.

I then explained a little about my deadly methods and how he could get bigger fish if he'd wade a little deeper, use a bigger fly and fasten it to a bigger rod. He thanked me graciously and smiled benignly. He could tell, he said, that I really had the Madison whipped. He shifted his slender bamboo rod and its well-worn English reel to the other hand.

"I certainly appreciate the information," he said. "I just don't fish for those big trout anymore."

I watched him go on upstream, wading skillfully and laying his line in soft, curling casts, and it occurred to me that not everybody is trying to break a world record. Since then, I have been the one with the little flies part of the time and I have been more reticent with instruction.

The Madison's variety of water types is accented by its lakes. Hebgen is just below the park's border, and the dam that holds it was built in 1916 to produce power. Then, just below Hebgen is Earthquake Lake, formed naturally by the quake of 1959, the one that altered an enormous landscape, changed Yellowstone National Park in more subtle ways and made a new fishery.

Then, below Ennis is Ennis Lake, also built for power and a

questionable addition to the system. Ennis Lake has silted heavily, become shallow and warmed its discharge water to the point that much of the Madison below it is very poor fishing in summer weather. Immediately below the dam is Bear Trap Canyon, a wilderness area with really wild water that requires skillful or foolish boatmen. Unlike some of the upper Madison, where more than 50 float boats are not unusual in a day, the Bear Trap has very few.

At times, the fishing there is excellent and I have watched spinfishermen take great catches of big brown trout when the river was too muddy for fly fishing. Below the Bear Trap the river smooths out a little; in fact, it is too wide for it suffers from hot sun. Some of the fine fly fishing there can end suddenly when the mercury climbs past the cutoff point and trout lose their appetite.

Fish management has been greatly affected by experiments made on the Madison. For years there was friction concerning hatchery trout over the entire West. One contention was that, even though they would not live long in the wild, hatchery trout would make fishing for the casual tourist and be good for business. But they were expensive and serious fishermen felt the money could be better spent in habitat improvement. In the late Sixties there was a research program on the Madison, involving the Montana Department of Fish, Wildlife and Parks. Dick Vincent, researcher, came up with the rather surprising information that hatchery trout when introduced to the Madison not only didn't survive long but that they caused drastic reduction in the numbers of wild trout. Reports of the Madison experiments may have done more than any other single project to alter the fish stocking programs of America.

The Madison, as Dan Bailey said, is a good neighbor to the Yellowstone, for it often can accommodate fishermen when the Yellowstone is muddy.

"At first, the Firehole does not look like a real river when you approach it in late fall. It looks like one of those overdone scenes in science fiction movies."

SIX

The Firehole

At first, the Firehole does not seem like a real river when you approach it in late fall. It looks like one of those overdone scenes in science fiction movies. There at Muleshoe Bend, for example, you'll have a readymade backdrop for a man in funny white clothes and carrying a raygun. Or you could use it for a scene of new arrivals in Heaven — or the other place.

The steam rises from a dozen little hot springs and bubbly mud pots, and from the river itself when it's cold in early morning. The steam freezes on riverside bushes and nearby trees and when the sun comes up they glitter in what is plainly a fake setup. Then a little air movement clears a spot over the sliding, weaving current and a trout rises silently, the circles widening from his bulge. Silent though it is, it must be a good fish. Early and late seasons are best on the Firehole. In midsummer it gets too warm. Early and late you can take your thermometer and find the temperatures that you and the trout like best.

The insects can find the temperatures that suit them too. The icy water on this side of the river folds into the steamy stuff from the seep across the way, and somewhere in between the temperature is just right. The insects come up, generally little ones, and dry their wings if the trout give them time. There may be a pod of fish working industriously here when the rest of the visible river has no action at all.

I'll go back to Charlie Brooks, the Yellowstone angling sage, who says his records show that the river is not as good as it used to be — not from fishing pressure but from too much warmth. A change in the weather?

No, some sort of change in the amount and temperatures of the springs and geysers that feed the river, part of the eerie results of the many earthquakes that have shivered the park in recent years — possibly releasing more heat from far down in the earth. Charlie Brooks is a long-time temperature taker of the river and although lately come fish managers may ignore his pronouncements he has time on his side — almost 40 years of time that hardly any ichthyologist has worked with. They would have retired too soon.

And just where do you take the river's temperature? It must be in the same place through the years because on a given day there are places where the water burns your hands and sometimes places where it chills your bones through waders, heavy pants and wool socks. Anyway, Brooks says the fish do not grow as large as they used to and he blames the longer periods of water too warm for growth. I go with him and his thermometer.

On one of those fall mornings just before the season closes you feel alone because the steam can cut off a long view, and when I first fished there late in the year, crunching snow along the banks, there was nobody fishing except our party. That has changed, I'm afraid. The word got out. And there are those who say some of the best of the Firehole comes when there's nobody fishing there at all. Winter.

But the fishermen scattered along the Firehole in fall or early summer make little impression upon the Canada geese that honk mildly as they curve into landings nearby. Buffalo and elk are there too. In September the bull elk bugle romantically and grunt with vulgar connotations.

Your Firehole expert knows things and tries things most fishermen never heard of. He'll check the mouth of Iron Creek to see if the fish are stacked up there deciding whether they want warmer or colder water. He'll use his thermometer and he knows he deals in a special river. It is a strange river with its own rules or lack of them.

There was the year when we had the cruising fish over on the stretch by the old freight road. That's somewhat away from the hot and cold tributaries and the temperature there has pretty well evened out. I saw some rises in a small section of water but couldn't get a strike. As usual when such things occur I pronounced to myself that they were taking something "too little to match." I kept circling my little group of fish and then realized they were moving. The light struck the water exactly right and there were more than a dozen burly rainbows, heading upstream, coming five feet from my waders.

Only a few minutes later another group passed me slowly, feeding on something I couldn't see. Infinitesimal nymphs worked before their noses got no results. Tiny dries got nothing, even though the fish broke the surface occasionally. Another group came along, apparently all rainbows.

I thought I saw quite a number of those traveling schools —but it may be the same ones showed up more than once as they semed to move either up or downstream. I never had a strike from them, and although fishing writers always seem to solve such problems, nothing worked for me. I saved the day, however. I saved it several times.

I went upstream to where the water was broken and came over some underwater rocks in bouncy waves and I cast a big Goofus Bug (it's called a *humpy* in some places) blind where the water began to level into more placid current. A rainbow struck it with a whack, and when I had landed him I felt better and went back to the schools of mystery fish. A fruitless hour of that and I went again to the riffle and caught another fish, realizing I was indulging in a childish procedure best kept quiet. I still haven't caught one of the pod fish and still don't know what they were looking for or if they were finding it. I must relate another Firehole performance.

Fred Terwilliger, Chester Marion and I went up into that country on the final day of the season several times and always caught fish, even if they ran a bit small sometimes. On one such trip we ended up on the stretch by the old freight road and found the river dimpled with constantly rising fish, most of them near the center. Fred began to fish the risers and didn't do much good. They were on small flies and I guess he never matched them. Since I have watched Fred catch plenty of Firehole fish on other occasions, I managed no deep pity for him. I felt artistic and began to photograph him with a background of buffalo that were wading the river downstream and close enough that Fred was having a little trouble concentrating.

I had never seen so many fish working on the Firehole — and never seen them so hard to catch. Marion made a few casts at them and then threw a fly tight against the bank where there were no rises at all. I suspect he'd seen a bubble or other movement there. Anyway, he hooked a good brown trout — something around two pounds — and released it with what I thought was smugness. But since I was only trying to take pictures and wasn't fishing at all, I forgave him his manner.

Casting to the bank he caught another brown, and another, all of them much larger than the fish feeding in the river's center. From where I sat I could see the mid-river risers. Marion continued to catch good ones, a dozen or more really fine specimens of around two pounds or so, none of them seeming to rise before he cast. It was not a true undercut bank and they were in barely enough water to cover them. As he got onto the business, Marion began to detect little movements back there. He was catching no small fish at all. He called it one of his best Firehole days, never figured what the fish were doing, why there were no small ones back there, or why they didn't show interest in what the smaller fish were consuming in mid-river. This, he agreed, was one of those Firehole things. I have sneaked back there several times since and felt silly casting into eight inches of still water against a bank. I never caught anything. I went back to a riffle where the fish were more indulgent.

I do not say the Firehole can always accommodate me when I fail in the tough stretches, simply that there are many kinds of water in it.

This one is strictly a Yellowstone Park fishery, rising there and joining the Gibbon at Madison Junction, forming the famous Madison — and consider that if someone had named things differently the whole thing might have been the Firehole or Gibbon instead of the Madison. Perhaps the most unusual thing about these beautiful rivers is that they are so available. In many places you could cast from your car although it would be rather silly.

"Your Firehole expert knows things and tries things most fishermen never heard of."

"On the way back we pulled over to look at Middle Creek, a tumbling roadside decoration."

SEVEN

Middle Creek

"In this country," Dan Bailey said, "almost everything is trout water. If it doesn't dry up in drought or freeze solid in winter or simmer in summer, there'll be trout."

That was a pretty long trout statement for him but the idea is intriguing and there is a special joy in catching trout where nobody is likely to try for them. Take Middle Creek, over there toward the eastern entrance of Yellowstone Park. Pretty hard to find boot tracks there.

It was a good fishing time and traveling anglers were running to and from all of the better known rivers and places like Soda Butte Creek. On that particular day I was sick and fed up with Soda Butte. Even among trout fishermen there are boors, pigs and congenital jerks. For some reason a gaggle of them had descended upon poor little Soda Butte, a pretty creek that runs through a piece of Montana and through some Yellowstone Park meadows before joining the Lamar River, that often cursed source of creamed coffee mud for the Yellowstone. Soda Butte sneakily contributes a little mud too now and then.

We have fished Soda Butte for years and the jerks looked like any other tourist fishermen at a distance. They crowded me out of a pool so I headed for another good one about 250 yards away. This outraged the pinheads who felt I was taking advantage of them, I guess. Four of them overtook me at a run, lined up at the pool like defensive linemen and glared menacingly. Since there isn't all that much of Soda Butte, I morosely joined my wife Debie and we went to Cody to visit the Buffalo Bill Museum.

On the way back we pulled over to look at Middle Creek, a tumbling roadside decoration. I have long known that pretty pictures of poor trout water are sometimes better received by editors than photos of more productive but less gurgly habitat.

"Stay up here on the road," I told Debie, "and take a picture of me down here in that sunny spot. I'll pretend I'm fishing in that little pocket to the right."

So I put on a Royal Wulff that I could see in the foam and bubbles, got in the right position and asked Debie if she were ready. She was so I slapped the fly on the pool under the fallen tree where there was hardly enough water to cover a muffin and most of the bottom came up and engulfed the fly. With consummate skill I set the hook hard enough to drive it into a brass bootjack and the tippet parted. I never got the cowardly big one back for another go-round but I caught a couple of pretty nice rainbows out of the puddle, and gleefully related my experience to Dan.

"Yes," he said mildly. "I've had a lot of fun on Middle Creek."

I think there was once when we caught fish in some sort of ditch-like creek near Helena and learned that Dan thought he had never been there. But then, there was no name for the thing as far as I know and I couldn't describe it very well. Maybe he just didn't recognize my description.

"It was a small dam, one of those that seems to have no important purpose other then building practice."

EIGHT

Sheep Creek

Like the rest of Smith River tributaries, Sheep Creek is missed by tourists with their eyes on spectacular mountain ranges and traveled anglers will never revere it as they do the Battenkill or the Firehole. It has the wrong name for there are simply too many Sheep Creeks. A Sheep Creek has no more chance of becoming famous than a Cow Creek has, no matter how many trout it supports or how spectacular its insect hatches.

This Sheep Creek is more than 30 miles long and it changes from valley stream to rocky canyon torrent and back again. Such waters are continually being rediscovered because no one writes books about them and there are no famous resorts to attract internationally famous fishermen and their rapt retinues. Nobody is likely to present an angling seminar on a Sheep Creek.

I never fished Sheep Creek with Dan Bailey and I realize now that I wasn't actually with him at very many of the fishing spots he directed me to. Not that it made much difference whether you rode in the same car with him or not. He was generally around the bend or across the ridge from his fishing friends anyway.

When he directed me to Sheep Creek he said there was good beaver pond fishing. There were brookies, rainbows, cutthroats and browns, he said. He always liked beaver ponds, even though such fishing might be scorned by technical anglers who sought specimen nymphs with little nets and avoided places where a Payne bamboo might be endangered by willows.

I found the tracks where Dan had parked his trailer and I started up the creek as Dan had advised. At first I waded in gravel-bottomed valley pools that were protected by so many willows and were strung in such a crooked pattern that I could work out barely enough line to avoid the degradation of simply dapping my fly with the leader, a process which could have been handled better with a canepole. Not that I was using any gem of the rodmaker's art. Long experience in Dan Bailey's wader tracks had taught me that many of his fishing spots were natural testing laboratories for anything a trout fisherman used and his searches for beaver ponds often went where the trout barely could.

Sheep Creek was good that day. I'd find miniature rapids where one pool fed into the next and where there would invariably be a turn in the stream's course, gouging a little undercut. There would be a gravelly bar next to the deeper channel and bubbles would parade down from the riffle's head. I'd flip the hair-winged Royal Wulff just below the rough water and watch it come down with the bubbles. If it outdistanced them or lagged behind it was a sign of drag, of course, but it could generally be mended enough to look as natural as a gaudy imitation of nothing in particular could be made to look, and the rainbows, browns and brook trout would come darting from the shadowy undercut area or rise menacingly from the gravel bottom. They weren't very big but a 10-incher in such quarters fits his environment and once he is hooked presents a landing problem in a stream six feet wide with willow roots and undercuts.

When I came to the first beaver pond I looked for a place to cast from. It was a small dam, one of those that seems to have no important purpose other than building practice. Already I could see bigger dams above it and I looked for a place to stand so that I could cast from below it to the rather sluggish current above. When I was ready I saw that I was literally standing in Dan's wader tracks, made the week before, and I felt flattered that he too had chosen that spot to cast from. I caught two rainbows in that little pond.

"You might have to hunt a way through some of that flooded bottom," Dan had said, "but there are some really good ponds as you work your way up."

I interpreted this as meaning much of the terrain was impassable. I went anyway.

The beaver dam pattern and its accompanying bog became a little confusing and I shipped a little water in my waders but I finally reached the biggest pond of the series. I raised my head very slowly from below the dam as if I were looking for an enemy gun emplacement instead of a 10-inch trout. The big pond was fairly new and had flooded willows and some small cottonwoods — even a pair of little pines. My head went up another six inches and instinctfully ducked back as a bunch of mallards slapped their way into the air.

The path of the original stream showed plainly, curving through the pond, but there was only a trace of current with a shimmering wind riffle. Dan said he'd used a little Muddler in that place but I stuck to the big hairwing and my first cast brought a fish, a good-sized rainbow, and then on the second cast there was a bulge and a wake from off in the flooded bushes and I caught a really good brook trout. Then I caught a somewhat smaller brown and stood there telling myself that I was a wonderful fisherman and that there must be thousands of such seldom-fished places — enough to last me for the rest of my life.

On one side of the beaver ponds was a rocky ridge and on the other side was a flat considerably higher than the creek. On the flat were tepee rings, loose stones laid in circles to fit the bases of a cluster of Indian wigwams. Perhaps they had been there for a hundred years in that logical place from which to watch the creek valley and another valley with another creek. It is disturbing to think that a single pickup truck could carry all of them away, removing a century or more of history in a few minutes. Dan had said they were a landmark to use in finding the beaver ponds and he accepted them for that as he would have accepted a rancher's mailbox or the buffalo jump over on Smith River itself.

Only a few years later most of the beaver dams washed out, bequeathing their collections of silt to the valley floor. Beaver ponds long gone have left meadows in the place of rocky ground through much of the world. Later, another generation of beavers surveyed Sheep Creek and stubbornly began a new system of ponds and spillways.

The creek begins its more than 30 miles in the Castle Mountains near King's Hill south of Great Falls. We camped up there once and followed it into a canyon where the fish were small and the pocket water swift and shallow.

At one point, just above the canyon, there is an access area with a willow bog and I managed to work my way into it from below, surprised to find some deep pools along the main creek. I bungled a good rainbow trout in there, glared at the widening circles where I had broken him off, and took a shortcut toward camp. I couldn't see out and I kept finding places too deep for my waders. Fact is, I got my directions a little mixed up in a sort of small-scale jungle and finally yelled for my wife Debie, who was waiting dinner in camp. She answered from an embarrassingly short distance but it was another ten minutes before I sneaked out to solid grassy ground.

Having fished both bog and canyon I was anxious to tell Dan about it and I did so at the hotel coffee shop. I thought he might want to try that part of the creek, even though the fish weren't very big. He filled his pipe.

"The canyon sure is pretty," he agreed, "but you have to be careful at the upper end. You can get stuck in that bog."

"Wrap late fall fly fishing into a big package and it is the Missouri River."
(Red Monical throws a big streamer in October.)

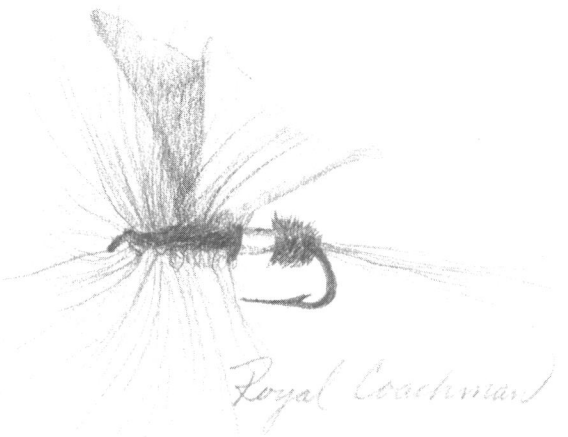

NINE

The Missouri

Wrap late fall fly fishing into a big package and it is the Missouri River. It is hard for Midwesterners to realize that the great muddy thoroughfare is a trout stream where it leaves the mountains.

When the keelboats of more than a century ago labored up it and the buffalo herds tried to cross it, sometimes with tragic results, it probably would have been hard to imagine a fancy fisherman with his vest of pockets and his split bamboo working a riffle or throwing a big streamer at a deep pool.

It begins as a full-blown river where the Madison, Jefferson and Gallatin join at Three Forks and if it weren't for the dams it would be just a big river of warm water fish for the most part, but in this case the dams have helped the trout — dams named Toston, Hauser and Holter, spilling cold water into good fishing sections where we can wade or drift and many of the fish are big.

Dam fighting trout anglers must make exceptions of rivers like the Missouri and the Big Horn. The Missouri is famous for big browns and rainbows, fish that weren't even living in Montana when the keelboats toiled upstream with their load of trade goods and their squint-eyed watchers for hostile Indians.

Big rivers are divided into little slices by dry fly fishermen in most cases. Side channels are better for the delicate touch and when Pat Barnes of Helena says he's going dry fly fishing on the Missouri he probably does it in little riffles apart from the main current much of the time, but if he uses a drift boat he can fish the shoreline as he goes down. Summer fly fishermen use the Missouri but they are less heard from than those who wade deep and throw far for the big brown trout that follow their spawning urge up from the big reservoirs in fall. Make it late September.

There at Beaver Creek, one of the best known fall spots of 20 years ago, the fishing seemed best when the mountain's shadow fell on the big pool in late afternoon. You might catch a big trout at any time but the shadow was a real omen, and often there would be heavy splashes as pre-spawners leaped far out in the middle where the slide of water was blurred by sunken boulders. The flies we threw were designed for such fish, hardly what traditional trout anglers sort over in their little boxes. We threw things to match the fish, flies as big as those used for striped bass or even tarpon. We threw them with big rods and considerable body English and the double haul was a way of life. Today's streamer throwers cast farther with better tackle but there are more scientific anglers today, preferring a more delicate touch most of the time.

When I first fished there at Beaver Creek, Dan Bailey was just getting started with the heavy fishing. He grumbled gently about it, saying now and then that he really was a small stream fisherman and that this was very unusual but he supposed he should do it. At first he continued to use the long, open loop needed for distance with a double-tapered line, but soon he leaned into his casts and threw shooting heads and monofilament backing. There at Beaver Creek we were just getting into the spirit of using steelhead tactics for brown trout.

The fly fishermen started it but spinfishermen adapted the big flies to appropriate lead sinkers and did as well or better. The flies tended to be offshoots of the Muddler Minnow as promoted by Bailey's store but I can't say any particular pattern was the big winner. Since then, there have been thousands of variations on the burr-headed sculpin imitation — or grasshopper imitation, or whatever it is.

The biggest fish I caught that fall was taken on what I called a Silver Doctor streamer that I had gotten from Dr. Ralph Daugherty for salt water, but Dan eyed it wryly and commented that "we don't tie Silver Doctors that way." A little crushed that I was using a cross-bred streamer, I named it the Silver Outcast and it appears under that name now and then in various fly fishing documents. But it is without honor, even though it has taken things like tarpon, snook, seatrout, black bass, rainbow trout and quite a few good browns. It is hard to get others to use it since it is obviously devoid of tradition or dignity. I have a special respect for it because Daugherty handed it to me in an Everglades Creek where he was fishing with the late Rocky Weinstein and our skiffs met in close quarters. Things like that make flies more important.

There have been good trout where Beaver Creek enters the Missouri for no one knows how long, but the big year was 1962, simply because fly fishermen seemed to gravitate to the spot at the time. Stand in that cold water long enough and you'd get a wallfish.

"There have been good trout where Beaver Creek enters the Missouri for no one knows how long, but the big year was 1962—"
(Dan Bailey fishes for his scales before releasing a trout over 5 pounds.)

The shadow moves across the river slowly and the big fish takes with a tug somewhere down near the bottom. Then you try to get your line on the reel and I noticed that some of the fishermen giggled inanely. A 4-pound fish wasn't anything great that year and there were sixes and sevens and at least one 10-pounder. That one was caught by Gene Anderegg, once a tournament caster, and he was with Bill Browning, then the outdoor promoter for the Montana Chamber of Commerce. It was a pretty fish and a pretty picture.

As I recall, most of the Beaver Creek fish were caught on floating lines at that time, but it was then that the shooting head was about to become popular for late-fall fishing. Steelhead tackle, all right. We wanted distance and we got it with gear developed by West Coast tournament casters and steelheaders, often the same people. It was Jim Green and Phillip C. Miraville who started the whole thing by winning casting tournaments with monofilament running line, beginning in 1946.

Traditionalists said it wasn't fly casting and Joe Brooks didn't like the idea but he finally went to it, even using a stripping basket made from a cardboard box to begin with. The deep-running lines that began to appear were liked better than lead sinkers for getting a streamer or giant nymph to the bottom. And distance? The magic 100 feet became just another cast.

Some floods damaged the Beaver Creek section later on, but undoubtedly there are other places just as good. Sometimes it can be shoulder-to-shoulder fishing near the dams in the fall. That's too bad because it isn't what we go West for.

Dan Bailey stood hip-deep in the Missouri and steered a 5-pound fish to a sand bar.

"They sure are big," Dan said. "Everything is out of proportion."

TEN

The Gallatin

He said he'd show us a new spot to fish and it was the first time we went fishing with Dan Bailey. We started at mid-afternoon and picked him up at the store in Livingston. Dan would show the way and we'd furnish the transportation, a brand new 4-wheel drive carryall type I was proud of.

We'd go to the Gallatin River, Dan said, certainly no secret stream, but he said there weren't very many fishermen where we headed. There sure weren't. We went west of Bozeman and I tried to find the exact spot later but couldn't. Dan took us there almost 30 years ago.

When Dan told me to stop driving we were on a pretty good back road but there was no water in sight. The river, Dan said, was down in there, pointing into a forest. Debie and I were glad we had someone who knew the way and we followed Dan through an intricate and pathless route through timber and finally willows. The Gallatin was there all right, clear and fairly low and easily crossed. Dan said he'd go upstream and we could work the other way. He wasn't talking much as we reached the water and I later learned that was Dan's typical anticipatory silence. No use jabbering when fishing was coming up.

Debie went off downstream and Dan and I stood and looked at a small pool with a rocky riffle at its head, a riffle that formed a classic "corner" with a slick somewhat above. Now before I go further, let me establish my trout fishing status at the time.

I'd fished trout for years with indifferent success and no personal instruction, and although Dan was obviously in a hurry to get started I asked him to show me the best trout lies in the water before us.

He indicated that anything he could show me was known to anyone who had visited a trout stream more than once but, after all, he could instruct and fish at the same time. He lengthened his line a little and laid a Number 14 dry fly where a little ridge of current leveled out into the still pool.

"That's a good place," he said.

Then he tried the other side of the little ridge of current. "And there," he said. Then there was a subtle change in his expression and tone and I realized Dan was now talking to himself as much as to me.

"And there!" he grinned, trying the other side of the riffle. "And there," sliding the line farther and putting the fly in the slick above the riffle, lifting his rod tip to extend the drift.

The rainbow was about 10 inches long and appeared beneath the fly, drifting along with it. I couldn't tell where it had come from. It was just there where it hadn't been before. It stared at the perfectly cocked fly and then sank a couple of inches — then disappeared.

"I guess he didn't want it after all," Dan said, laughing as if the refusal had been better than a take. "And there." The last, "and there", punctuated a cast that went farther upstream and descended near the shoreline and a clump of willows.

"I'll see you after a while," Dan said, and disappeared around the willows so quickly and silently that I made some inane remark no one heard. I turned and looked at the stream, actually little more than a creek, for we were in a side channel, and cast a Number 16 Adams at the spot where the rainbow had refused Dan's fly, but it didn't come back.

There were several splits in the little river there and I wasn't quite sure just where Debie had gone. I began fishing carefully but without result, changing flies with the crafty anticipation of the amateur who feels the right bit of feathers will change an entire day. And although I would like to tell you about the results it was a long time ago and, frankly, I don't remember whether I caught any fish or not.

Since it was the first time I had gone fishing with Dan Bailey I supposed he would come back downstream at any moment, but he didn't. After fishing around for a while and probing cautiously into a split or two I ran into Debie, who was working back upstream. The low sun was throwing the shadow of a ridge and suddenly it began to get pretty dark. We wondered what had become of Dan. Up to then I had paid no attention to where we were, having relied on him to lead us back to the truck.

"Maybe," I suggested, "we should start back on our own." We did. The west was still fairly light and that's the general direction we'd come from. Since we didn't have a compass it seemed a good idea to go back through the willow jungle while there was still

some light to follow. Debie walked ahead and I carried the rods, butt forward. Then I began to get in a hurry, having no desire to spend the night with the Gallatin River, a forest of underbrush and busy mosquitoes. I went up ahead of Debie and began to break through the brush instead of threading around it for I wanted to keep my course as straight as possible. One of the rods caught on something and I pulled off a guide. The rods were glass, not particularly expensive, and were used for back country fishing. Believe me, although we weren't far from the road, we were in back country. We hurried faster as the light faded. We'd taken the wrong angle toward the truck.

The sky was only a little brighter in the west when we finally came to a steep climb, which had to be the way up to the road. We crawled up it and came to the road but had no idea which way to go to reach the truck.

"I think we kept bearing right," Debie said. "Let's head to the left."

It was no more than half a mile before we found the shiny new truck, parked on the road cut out of the bluff. Dan wasn't there. We waited for a few minutes, then nosed the rig toward the river somewhere below and turned on the headlights, their beams dissolving in the empty night except for reflection from a few insects. We waited a while longer and there was a rustling in the bushes. Dan climbed out and lighted his pipe.

"We turned on the lights because we thought you might need some help to make the highway," I said apologetically, fearful lest he might be offended at any suggestion he was misplaced in the "familiar" Gallatin Valley.

"You did the right thing," Dan said. "I always get lost when I go down there."

Now there is no suggestion that Dan Bailey was a back country incompetent. He simply didn't care much where he was when fishing and tended to wait until dark before deciding how to get back to camp or car. In that one trip I learned that Dan's guiding was from camp or car to fishing water. From then on you were on your own. To him, fishing was a personal thing to be done primarily alone and even if he went with a crowd he liked to fish by himself.

The Gallatin was a pet river of Dan's, especially the lower parts, which are largely on private property. Perhaps it is not a "tourist" river there. I have gone to several spots on the lower East and West Gallatins, following Dan's instructions, and seldom found much competition from other fishermen. But the lower Gallatin often suffers from the withdrawals of irrigation water.

The West Gallatin (sometimes called the "main" Gallatin) rises in Yellowstone National Park and it has its own lake up there.

The cold water comes from snows. Between West Yellowstone and Gallatin Gateway far downstream the river is a roadside creek with innumerable pullouts. It's easily fished but the trout, mostly rainbows, are generally small. We've tried it at intervals for years and only recently began to watch the temperatures.

A West Yellowstone guide once told us he was having fine fishing a few miles downstream and we tried it one morning when everything looked like tourist folder scenes. We waded in hip boots with felt soles, working areas easily crossed. It's mostly swift and riffly. We caught nothing and went back to West Yellowstone for lunch. Then we tried it around 2 p.m., and things had changed. The sun had warmed and the trout were busy and a little bigger than we'd expected. Debie, perched on a boulder near the road, hooked a bigger fish than she thought could live there, but it got away. On the upper Gallatin and its little tributaries a thermometer can be helpful. But nothing is a sure thing and a year later we caught only the small fish we'd learned to expect there. I am not touting the area for record seekers.

Down in the East Gallatin there was some quiet fishing water that slipped through ranch land and later through surburban homes spreading out from bustling Bozeman. When Dan first directed me to a place on the East Gallatin I'm not sure I went to exactly the spot he described. It was "somewhere back of the cheese factory." I went there several times, always in late evening, and for some reason I went alone.

There were cottonwoods and a cottontail rabbit that I invariably met at dusk. The river was slow and never extremely clear and there were deep places that nudged the tops of my waders. Usually, there was no one else there but on one evening I recall some spinfishermen.

I had waded into a deep bend where a little pod of fish were dimpling. I watched them a little while before casting to them and I identified a whitefish, then saw the blunt nose of a trout. The trout had either misjudged carelessly or had taken something different from the dimpling targets. Aha!

I cast carefully and only a short distance to the busy area and a small whitefish gulped my Number 16 Cahill just as one of the spinfishermen came by.

"Those fish are all whitefish, mister," he said. "I can tell by the way they bite."

I thanked him but kept on casting after he had left and hooked a fat rainbow. Then I caught a brown trout and the working fish continued as night came on. I could barely see the rises and certainly couldn't see my tattered fly. Whitefish. Brown. Rainbow.

There was considerable splashing, my elbows in the water part of the time. The spinfishermen were leaving and passed only a few feet away.

"That guy sure is giving those little whitefish hell," said the one who had talked to me earlier. "I guess if you can't catch trout, whitefish are better than nothing. But he's using a fly rod. Flies sure catch whitefish."

There was just a little hook of a moon and my last brown trout was only a blob in the streak of light. I fumbled around and found the fly in his jaw. It was a wonderful evening.

Far up the Gallatin, not far from Sage Creek, things were different when I went there to photograph the beginning of a stream. The Gallatin itself there is a good-sized river, of course, but it is fed by some little mountainside trickles that could be called the beginnings of trout streams and I had some high-flown literary ambition of following Rocky Mountain snow water all the way to the ocean. I made pictures of spring and snow water coming down the steep slope. In chilly weather those trickles form ornate ice designs along their routes.

Beneath one little skein of trickles was a deep pool heavily bordered by watercress. I needed some action for a picture and Debie dutifully sloshed to the edge of the pool, which was somewhat higher than the river. She cast a dry fly into it and a fish took immediately. It was a brookie and considerably above the tiddler class. A continent away from their origin, the brook trout appear in hundreds of chilly little trickles and occasionally surprise a fisherman when coming up among browns and rainbows. But then, browns and rainbows are transplants too.

There are all kinds of trout along the Gallatin — at least most kinds.

ELEVEN

The Jefferson

"Sure I know about the Jefferson," the man said. "It connects the Beaverhead and Big Hole to the Missouri."

That's a common view of the Jefferson, which isn't the greatest trout stream in the world. It has escaped promotion and isn't very well known. I guess that was what Dan Bailey liked. When I asked people about the Jefferson they often said:

"I don't know much about it but Dan Bailey fishes over there."

Much of the Jefferson is slow moving, so slow in fact that drift fishermen are likely to spend considerable time on the oars and there are summer days when it's necessary to hunt for riffles where the water is aerated and the trout are moving. And at those times mornings and the evenings will be best.

Clear water can be a problem for the Jefferson is in irrigation country with murky returns and the Beaverhead brings in its silt. The banks shift with heavy rains. The mud bottoms of much of the river are avoided by careful fishermen. There are many splits with confusing channels.

Water temperatures can be high in late summer when water volume is robbed by irrigation. June and July are generally considered best and the successful fisherman must be a student as well as a caster. For the bigger trout, baitfish take the place of insect hatches that aren't plentiful. Bordered by roads and rails, the Jefferson is one of those lightly fished streams passed by fishermen headed somewhere else. Dan said it could be pleasantly lonely.

Since the water is slow the best fish are generally brown trout and it's sometimes necessary to "fish through" a barrier of whitefish to get at the trout. It isn't always easy to wade because banks are likely to be brushy and there are plenty of deep holes.

"Sure I know about the Jefferson," the man said. "It connects the Beaverhead and Big Hole to the Missouri."

Generally, the best water is supposed to be in the upper part where float trips are most common and there are more rainbows. Probably the best of Jefferson fishing comes in fall when the big browns move to shallow water and seek spawning gravel.

Here is a big and little known river, some 70 miles of it, and while headed somewhere else a traveling angler is likely to say, "Now, let's see. What river is that? This isn't the Missouri is it?"

It's quite a bit of the Missouri.

"The water below the Slough Creek Campground also holds both rainbows and cutthroat-rainbow crosses. Sometimes it is very delicate fishing."

TWELVE

Slough Creek

It is an uphill hike to the higher meadows of Slough Creek, going from a meadow stream upward to a canyon cataract and then to a meadow stream again. From the air the upper Slough Creek is seen to wander carelessly on a broad valley floor. It is back country but with a wagon road that goes to a single guest ranch — Silver Tip. The creek is in Yellowstone Park for some 16 miles of its length, coming out of the Beartooths not far from Cooke City.

Sometimes in midsummer the big, boldly-patterned cutthroats of the upstream meadows (the upper one is several miles from the trailhead) are almost too easy to take, gulping big dry flies, especially hopper patterns, with deliberate moves, and on calm days one can sometimes see the loafing fish he plans to catch on the next cast. Only energetic fishermen regularly make the trip to the upper meadow and back the same day. Camping is restricted but can be arranged by back packers or horse outfits. Occasionally, the Park Service warns of bears up there.

Downstream from the high meadows, below the rocky canyon, is a campground, often filled in early afternoon during midsummer, and below the campground is the rest of the meadow stream, running some distance with a few breaks before entering the Lamar on its way to the Yellowstone. Although the upper river is strictly a native cutthroat stream, the water below the campground also holds both rainbows and cutthroat-rainbow crosses. Sometimes it is very delicate fishing.

Having stopped to rest one afternoon after being duped by those downstream fish, I was passed by polite strangers from the East. Fishing wasn't good, they smiled, so I condescendingly explained to them that the fish could be temperamental there, sometimes taking very small flies. I assumed, of course, that they had come from easier Park waters.

"Oh, yes," they said. "We found we had to go to 8-X tippets and Number 22 flies. We make Slough Creek every year."

Since 8-X tippets and Number 22 flies give me some eye and finger trouble these days, I resolved not to be authoratative toward strangers. I recalled another time when I had given some tips to a youngster who seemed to be hanging on my every word at Slough Creek. After expansively telling him what big fish I had caught in the upper meadows, I looked more closely at his tackle when he said he'd caught one up there that weighed "a little over eight pounds." I've never seen a Slough Creek cutthroat that big but I believe him.

Not far above the Lamar intersection the creek is quite wide, deep in places and sluggish. One sod bank is steep most of the way and the bigger cutthroats tend to live against it where it crumbles gradually in sections. Although it isn't a particularly long cast from the other side, it can be very difficult to get a good float unless you study current faithfully and watch the wind. Once, when no one was watching, I simply crossed over and, hiding behind the high bank, I made very short casts over the edge to rising fish. I caught them with considerable satisfaction — but began to feel it was sneaky not to cast from the easy side.

The native cutthroat is not the fightingest fish in that country but Dan always said the cutthroat could be as hard to fool as a brown trout under some conditions and I agree to that, even though some of the Upper Slough Creek fish seem to look me in the eye as they take my big dries.

Red Monical and I were having a fine day at Slough Creek until the trout ruined it in early afternoon. Red found a fairly swift run below the campground with constantly rising fish. Suddenly he wasn't catching them any more and while I watched sympathetically from the bank the trout came very near to a frenzy, churning the water almost like rampaging bluefish. Red went from big impression flies to some of the most dainty drys of the Bailey shop, to the small nymphs and back to the big Wulffs. The boiling trout ignored them and Red's only thrills came when he mistakenly tried to set the hook in an occasional fish that was taking something else beside his fly. The light was perfect and dozens of the risers could be seen plainly as they came up.

I tried a few but hooked nothing, so I wandered 40 yards up the creek, secretly feeling there would be no more fish — that all of them were tormenting Red. But I cast an Adams to a quiet backwater and a good cutthroat took it with the deliberate, fin-showing rise they are noted for. Then there was another and I looked back to where Red was still stubbornly going through his fly box.

Now Red Monical is a highly-skilled fisherman but I do not consider Slough Creek the most difficult stream most of the time. I must insist that Slough Creek can be tough and that cutthroats can change suddenly and begin to act surprisingly like educated brown trout on certain days.

In fall there is no other stream that turns off the way Slough Creek does. Once the water reaches a cutoff temperature and holds it, I find it difficult to believe all those trout are still in there. I look down through cold clarity and see nothing move. If they were really there, I tell myself, I could see them. They must, I used to say, drop down into the Lamar. But that's not true. I think they are still there and perhaps "semi-dormant" is not too strong a term.

So I reel in my line and look off up the slope where an unseen coyote is beginning to tune for his evening yodeling. Maybe that is what starts the bull elk bugling somewhere up there in the timber patch, even if the height of the rutting season is over. Those are Canada geese that go down the creek with conversational honking. I decide I'd better head back down Paradise Valley toward Livingston where the water's a little warmer and the brown trout are lighted up for fall.

"The Boulder comes by its name naturally and much of the bottom is made up of jumbled rocks—"
(caster is Mary Kefover Kelly, angling historian.)

THIRTEEN

Boulder River of the Yellowstone

Trace the Boulder River of the Yellowstone from the air and you see it gather itself in the Absaroka peaks a little north of Yellowstone Park. It runs northward. There are small, high lakes there and the light airplane goes between gigantic mountain shoulders, then into the Boulder canyon and valley.

No river of the area is more dramatic in its beauty and when a pilot swings his plane in a curve above the Natural Bridge his passengers will gasp. The Natural Bridge and its accompanying waterfall form a natural division of the Boulder's trout population. The bridge is part of a precipitous canyon section and if summer water flow is normal, part of the river runs over it into a booming falls and part of it flows under it to make another cataract.

Below the Natural Bridge there are brown trout as well as rainbows and cutthroats and big fish work upstream from the Yellowstone, which the Boulder joins a little below Big Timber. Above the falls the fish run somewhat smaller and the brown trout are absent.

In the upper part the Boulder is sensitive to cold weather, its season being much shorter than that of the lower river, which resembles the Yellowstone itself in seasons. A few miles of exposure to sun makes the difference and the lower river has its insect hatches to please experienced fishermen.

The Boulder comes by its name naturally and much of the bottom is made of jumbled rocks that some rueful waders have called "greased cannonballs" at a time of year when considerable algae collects on stones that would be difficult wading at best. But other areas are quite comfortable for felt soles.

So there is some 50 miles of Boulder. Make it both East and West Boulder or "Main Boulder" and West Boulder. The two streams join at McLeod about 16 miles upstream from Big Timber. There is a public fishing access there and another below Big Timber. The lower main Boulder is mainly private land and so are parts of the West Boulder and access varies from year to year and from rancher to rancher. Just above the Natural Bridge on the main Boulder the pavement gives way to gravel and it becomes National Forest country. The road is near the river almost all the way.

Hike upstream on the West Boulder and you'll reach high meadows in National Forest land, breaking out of heavy forest suddenly. There's often good fishing there although the hike is too easy to prevent considerable pressure.

Through the years the summer homes, guest ranches and campgrounds have closed in on much of the Boulder and the Baileys used to camp farther up, where Dan said the fish were smaller but the solitude greater. But he fished the lower river a great deal too.

After some miles on good gravel the track changes and the sign says it is "primitive," a little uncomfortable, even for some regular users of backwoods vehicles. On one of our first trips to the upper river we had a flat tire and worried until we got back to civilization on the spare. That was many years ago, and as I steered gingerly over jagged rocks and through cavernous chuckholes I swore never again to leave civilization in any truck without two spares. I lived up to that oath, and although I have never used the second one, no matter how foolishly I wandered into the unknown, the extra tire has done wonders for my morale.

Dan said the main or East Boulder didn't have very good fishing after he got up to where it was only a trickle to be fished in leather boots, and that was our experience too, but we've had fun with plenty of smaller fish somewhat above the weekend crowds. Sometimes the water has been so clear that an overhead color photograph hints the fisherman wasn't standing in water at all.

Independence is a ghost settlement we stared at during a snowstorm — the remains of what was once a mining community, and we were hushed as we stood in one of the buildings and examined the payroll records of another era, the brittle paper having withstood generations of cold and heat. Crumbled log houses were nearby. But the mine was located much farther up than a fisherman needs to go and somewhat past the best fishing.

On one trip we'd tent-camped for the night near the river's beginnings and drove bouncily back downstream to where there seemed plenty of water to really cast, and I threw a Muddler Minnow across the river against a shore that seemed slightly undercut in places. First was a cutthroat and the second cast brought a rainbow, both more than a foot long. Red Monical

cheered and strung his rod. We went back many times after that. All of the Baileys camped on the upper Boulder from time to time, and it became a favorite place of John's.

There's true wilderness country available from the upper Boulder, hunting parties staging their horse outfits at Independence on the way to elk country, and bears sometimes come down from the untracked heights to pester campers. On one of our earlier trips a black bear hung around camp persistently, making us a little nervous, for even the clownish black can be dangerous when he becomes addicted to camp garbage.

At dusk another party unrolled their sleeping bags a little distance away and I thought it best to mention to them that the bear was persistent. One of the newcomers responded by leaning a Mannlicher near their fire. It was quite late that night when the bear came back, showed interest in one of the sleeping bags and its contents and brought the camp wide awake. He left at top speed, showering gravel against the side of our tent and urged on by the Mannlicher, which flashed brightly and boomed especially loudly in the small hours. We didn't rest well after that.

As you go farther upstream the forest begins to close in and the summer homes and ranches seem farther away than they really are.

"Drifting the Beaverhead is no white water adventure but the thing winds and hurries so that it is easy to end up against a bank with your oar groping in the willows."
(Tom Morgan with Dan Bailey.)

FOURTEEN

Beaverhead River

On the upper Beaverhead River, which runs rapidly through a corridor of willows and tends to forego the traditional trout stream pattern of pool, riffle and pool again, it is easy to end up with a sore elbow and wrist. The first time I slid down through a section of it with Bill Browning and an efficient guide from Dillon I kept feeling we were passing up more water than we were fishing and that the best plan would be to keep going back through the same route until we'd really worked it over.

Some of the hardest work in fly casting is to belabor a shoreline at close range from a moving boat. You cannot cast rapidly enough to cover all of the water you need to and as you go along you cast faster and faster and invariably feel that you could have done better with a different rod and line combination.

Browning and I launched an inflated boat and did some fishing without a guide. We still went too fast but we still caught fish. There aren't very many really good wading spots on the upper Beaverhead. The river runs about 50 miles from where it begins below Clark Canyon Dam, joining the Big Hole at Twin Bridges, after picking up the Ruby along the way.

Downstream from Dillon (going north) the Beaverhead deals with civilization in the form of heavy irrigation withdrawals and the silting effect of returned irrigation water. That is brown trout country but the river can be too hot or too cold as it goes broad and shallow through ranch meadows. It is good fishing but it requires study and application.

At Clark Canyon Reservoir I was just a little bored years ago when Bill Browning insisted that we try lake fishing. The running water below the dam interested me more and we'd been doing pretty well there. The reservoir, I thought, was more interesting as a duck hunting spot and I usually associate reservoir fishing with trolling. Bill said we'd cast big, weighted Girdle Bugs.

The Girdle Bug is one of the least aesthetic of trout nymphs, being an outgrowth of the Woolly Worm with waving rubber legs. As we drifted across underwater vegetation but in pretty deep water, I hand-twisted my Girdle Bug along on a sinking line, imagining I was making it look seductive down there in semi-darkness. When it stopped I set the hook, expecting a weed but finding something that moved fast. When the trout surfaced and Bill netted it, I decided a 6-pounder on a Girdle Bug was no disgrace after all.

Drifting the Beaverhead is no white water adventure but the thing winds and hurries so that it is easy to end up against a bank with your oar groping in the willows. To the disgust of more dainty operators I find that a heavily overloaded rod will slap a streamer against a bank on a short line much better than a matched outfit.

Years after Browning and I did it, Dan Bailey, who'd fished the Beaverhead from time to time, asked if I'd like to float it with him, Tom Morgan and another friend. Morgan, top angler and later to be owner of the Winston Rod Company in Twin Bridges, was the host and it seemed he had pretty well worked out the problems of spillway releases from Clark Canyon. The next day would be just right, he said.

When Dan and I arrived on the scene I noted that I was treated with rather cool courtesy and I finally decided the Beaverheaders thought Dan had brought a writing spy to reveal their water level expertise. When I finally convinced them that I would pen no revelations our relations thawed considerably.

We caught a great many trout that day and they were good fish, but I found that Tom, who was in the boat with me, did a lot better than I did. Without disparaging his skill I report that his outfit was better suited to the short shoreline casts than mine was. As I recall, the Muddler Minnow and its relatives were big winners that trip.

Access to the Beaverhead has been a troublesome thing and it has been the locale of violent disagreement between sportsmen and ranchers. More drift boats have added to fishing pressure, but the trout population remains very high.

Poindexter Slough at Dillon is a completely different kind of fishing, a meadow creek with islands of vegetation. It has a fishing access point and can be some of the most delicate fishing of the region, but cannot accommodate many rods at one time. It is not the easiest wading, not because of fast water or slippery rocks but because there are numerous sections almost blocked by unstable water growth.

Beaverhead country has attracted fewer tourists than areas nearer Yellowstone National Park. It is cow country and some of the smaller streams are little known. The Ruby and the Red Rock are followed by anglers who don't talk much about them. There's a fine Sheep Creek down by Lima and at a little lake called Deadman the trout felt dry flies were just fine. Deadman is a long drive from the highway and the Red Conglomerate Peaks above it mark the edge of Idaho.

"Poindexter Slough at Dillon is a completely diffrent kind of fishing, a meadow creek with islands of vegetation."

"But there are 150 miles of Big Hole River, fishing water of so many types it can match almost any other stream of the region."

FIFTEEN

Big Hole River

We went to the Big Hole to fish for grayling near the beginning of the South Fork. There were plenty of grayling there, Dan Bailey said, even though they didn't run very large. I'd never caught one and had failed on an earlier attempt or two. The Big Hole, we were told, was very nearly the only river system of the region that still held them.

We were using dry flies at dusk on ranchland not far from Wisdom and the little grayling came up briskly, along with some small rainbows and brook trout — not that there are no big fish on the upper Big Hole, but we simply didn't find them that day. On the other side of a willow clump I heard what seemed to be a cow grazing rather daintily and when I stepped past the willows I saw that it was one of a group of mule deer that moved away casually with no particular alarm. In winter, the deer sometimes came into the Wisdom saloon in those days, accepting handouts from the customers, standing comfortably on the sawdust floor.

The Wisdom saloon was a stubborn scrap of unchanged cow country and served good lunches. On the first day we visited it there was a single man resting at a big card table, his hat pushed back and his head on his arms. Another man came through the door, thumped his high-heeled boots across the sawdust and sat down directly opposite him. He picked up a deck of cards and riffled them absent-mindedly, looking closely at the sleeper.

"Mister," called the bartender, "it's a rule of the house. If you're gonna play cards with that man you have to wake him first!"

Fishermen didn't seem to be very plentiful around Wisdom that summer and lady casters were something of a novelty. My wife Debie, having caught some small grayling, was prospecting for bigger game.

"I know where there's some big trout," a man at the bar said, "and you can see them from a little knob over the river, but I'm damned if I know how to catch them. I tried everything."

Debie pricked her ears and began skilled interrogation coming from long experience. She asked if the man had tried artificial grasshoppers and he had. He had tried Woolly Worms, he said, and he had tried nymphs and a favorite wet fly he tied himself. He had even resorted to worms.

"Lady," he said. "I tried a 30-06 too, but that didn't work either."

In some of the upper Big Hole and its tributaries there are too many brook trout, a species that continually threatens itself through over-population and stunting.

But there are 150 miles of Big Hole River, fishing water of so many types it can match almost any other stream of the region. The lower parts are noted as drifting water. Most of the river is closely followed by a highway.

Along with the varied fishing the Big Hole has the varied problems of famous water. Like some other Montana streams it runs largely through ranch land and the subtraction of irrigation water has sometimes ruined late summer fishing below Glen. While environmentalists may explain that the river is worth more as a fishing stream than as an irrigation source, the receipts from fishing go into different pockets and a rancher who desperately needs water for his alfalfa is likely to have little sympathy for someone who collects tourist dollars. Compromise is a continuing Western program. There have been times on the Big Hole when bulldozers have changed an entire scene in a few minutes, and diversions can cause bank damage as well as bottom changes.

Salmon fly time in June is the big season for fishing and a good time for floating. The best of the river is a good size for casting at almost any water stage. It has the full complement of trout qualifications including shore and bottom cover and the classic succession of pools, splits and riffles.

From Divide to where it joins the Beaverhead at Twin Bridges, the Big Hole is listed as blue ribbon trout water, a designation carefully sought by some tourist fishermen and avoided by a few who grumble good-naturedly that such a classification causes overcrowding.

Above the settlement of Wise River, where the Wise River enters, is easily fished meadow water, a gentle stream of the kind sought by many travelers. It is sometimes said that from Divide to Glen is the classic section. The irrigation problems are below that.

This river is better known for stonefly and caddis hatches than for mayflies, and the current passion for the caddis as an all-around attraction means many fishermen will be well-equipped when they arrive.

In the best known stretches there can be boat congestion and one embittered wader warns that it's hard to be comfortable when you may be run over by a drift boat at any moment. It's an exaggeration for most of the season but there *are* crowded times and places, times when more than 50 boats are seen to pass a given point in a single day.

Joe Brooks, best known of the writers who watched fishing bloom in Montana, has listed it as one of the best of all trout streams, anywhere. The Big Hole *is* one of the best and the world knows it.

"It's easy wading in the main river there and when the Baileys arrived just before dusk, Dan would earnestly seek his breakfast trout and then release the rest."

SIXTEEN

Smith River

The Smith River is best known as a floater's stream, and although it can be rough, and even dangerous in high water there are times when canoes are nearly ideal, even for those of limited experience.

"It's more like the real Montana," John Bailey says as he drives back toward Livingston from White Sulphur Springs in gathering darkness. What he means is that the Smith is not in typical tourist country, and most of it is bordered by ranches or wilderness. Much of the upper part is rolling sage and grass country although the canyon stretches are as they were hundreds of years ago.

The last time I saw Helen and Dan Bailey camping they had parked their trailer at the Camp Baker access, from where floaters take off for 60 miles of drifting through rough country. The skimpily developed site is ideal for boat launching and is at the mouth of Sheep Creek, not far from the teepee rings that overlook the valley — and not far below the buffalo jump where Indians of another era drove wild-eyed bison to crashing death.

Strangely, when a parade of boats is thumping through the canyons, there may be few or no fishermen at the place most of them put in. People bent on several days of wilderness living usually have eyes mainly for their coming journey and seldom note that they are leaving some fine fishing. Dan Bailey would leave his trailer and wade into the little river 50 feet from where engrossed outfitters were packing their boats — big inflatables, McKenzies, johnboats and canoes. He'd cast a good-sized dry fly or a Muddler Minnow along the shore, going upstream, or he'd slip into the mouth of Sheep Creek. It's easy wading in the main river there and when the Baileys arrived just before dusk Dan would earnestly seek his breakfast trout and then release the rest.

Conservationists have worried about the Smith River. Some of the floaters who make the long trip below Camp Baker are not fishermen at all, but some of them are environmentalists bent on living from the land — and they eat more trout than do more serious anglers. The expert at survival is likely to employ the most practical methods and keep his fish, but the river seems to have withstood years of such operations.

There are some big trout at Camp Baker but most of them run around a foot long, fish that usually take scattered naturals, and it's seldom there is a well-defined hatch. It's a good place in late summer grasshopper season. When you catch a fish by the launching site the busy boatmen hardly look up.

The river usually runs low in late summer, partly from the demands of irrigation, and when the sign at the Camp Baker gate reports water is too skimpy for practical floating, only someone willing to push and pull a bit in the shallows should take off. Any boat used then should slide easily over rocks and a tight time schedule is difficult to keep. Later, as early fall comes on, the water may be a little deeper — and when it cools, fall can be some of the best of the Smith.

Below Camp Baker there are some deeper holes and classic pool and ripple sections where the trout, especially browns, are likely to be much larger, but some of the most entertaining fishing is even farther up than Camp Baker. Not far below Fort Logan there is a public access and campground where short-float anglers can put in for a one-day trip to Baker. We've often camped there and walked downstream to where the wader tracks disappear and past the abandoned homestead site to where there are some willow-lined deep holes.

Farther down toward Camp Baker the road swings near the buffalo jump, located near to a crumbling red cliff. The buffalo jump itself is just downstream from the red cliff and its efficiency as a deathtrap is obvious. Did those ancient Indians of the buffalo slaughter once camp at the confluence of the Smith and Sheep Creek?

The water above and below the jump is mostly fairly shallow but there are times when even the tiny streams that feed the river near there will have trout. In late summer the fishing generally becomes difficult, possibly to revive in fall. It is "upstream" fishing but it is far from the beginning.

Near White Sulphur the river appears more like a spring creek, which it mainly is, and there are north and south forks. The south fork passes by the old stage barn, not far from Ringling and a few yards from U.S. Highway 89. I didn't know what the sturdy old barn had been built for until Dan told me. A good place for brook trout, especially early in the season. At the little bridge just off the highway and a few yards from the unused building there are pools where brookies dimple the surface and disappear in little bottom mud swirls when I cast carelessly.

The prolific little brookies are taken by bucketfuls by fishermen who eat no other trout but consider them delicacies, and without the harvest they would be in stunted swarms.

Fishing by the stage barn is best in evening when there are quiet times with no audible traffic on the highway and it is easy to believe I can hear the curt orders of professionals as they hitch teams that will pull a creaking, swinging stagecoach in its dash along the valley.

When we leave the shining little stream, slow-going through its meadow, we will pass antelope on the hillsides and recall the time we shot the sage hens near Ringling. And then there were the brookies of tiny Battle Creek there and the fishing at Sixteenmile Creek. Good place for a short trip from Livingston, Dan said.

"Fishing by the stage barn is best in evening when there are quiet times with no audible traffic on the highway and it is easy to believe I can hear the curt orders of professionals as they hitch teams that will pull a creaking, swinging stagecoach in its dash along the valley."

SEVENTEEN

Bighorn River

The Bighorn River is different, regulated by the discharge from Yellowtail Reservoir, a big enough and deep enough lake to produce warmer water in winter and cooler water in summer. It runs through a part of Montana not usually considered trout country — at much lower altitude than the other famous rivers.

Yellowtail Dam is located not far from Hardin, and the trout water is from the dam down to Hardin. Beyond that the river becomes cloudy and its appearance begins to match other lowland cow country streams. It's near Hardin that the Little Big Horn enters, famous because of the Custer Battlefield.

Best and best known of the Bighorn water runs through the Crow Indian Reservation, the Crows having looked with disfavor upon outside anglers. The state opened the river to fishing in 1981, early reports indicating it was the greatest trophy trout river of the lower 48 states. From the first there was heavy fishing pressure and drift fishing prospered. Approach from the banks was limited and remains so, although there is hope for additional access areas.

The unprecedented fertility of the water made almost any kind of trout fishing successful. At first the desire for record fish made big streamers and big nymphs most popular. Then, after a year or so of fishing, a great many of the Bighorn fly casters took more advantage of surface hatches and small flies and nymphs prospered. Some of the favorites are tiny, seemingly more appropriate for meadow creeks than for tailwaters. A trophy fisherman of 1981 reported wonderingly that he had "laid down my big rod" and gone after a teeming hatch that raised a throng of 3-pound fish.

Fishing pressure undoubtedly reduced the catches of extremely large trout, but a change in method may have contributed too. The little flies with which anglers worked a variety of hatches and probed for shrimp and nymph seekers simply are not likely to bring the monsters. So catch figures and weights may be a little deceptive in this case. Drift fishermen still continued to rake the banks with streamers and hardware, however.

It is not a fast river, and level changes due to spillway control are not sudden enough to be dangerous, but float fishermen must watch for sunken timbers. There have been accidents, partly because of smooth currents that put the boatman off guard. And there are some special wading hazards which must be mentioned.

Most of the bottom seems disarmingly comfortable to fishermen who have slipped and lunged through the Madison or the Yellowstone, but there is so much water growth that the bottom is hard or impossible to see in spite of clear water. The abrupt dropoff of a gravel bar has put many waders in trouble. As in the case of the driftboater, the wader may feel falsely secure. A bit of white water and some roaring boulders might be a godsend to those who tend to forget their wading rules.

Call it a year-around fishery, but there are seasonal changes. November is one of the best months in most years, the water still warm enough on the Big Horn when it can get too cold on most regional streams — temperature tempered by the lake as well as low altitude (around 3000 feet). Fishing remains good into January and many a drift boat carries duck guns as well as rods.

Good hatches can be expected in May and June and the Bighorn temperatures become ideal rather late in summer when some trout water is warm enough that fishermen are looking forward to the fall cooldown. In midsummer there can be a paradox of cold water and uncomfortably hot air temperatures.

The future of Bighorn brown trout was once in doubt, a question of spawning gravels, but they seem to reproduce satisfactorily. Planted rainbows have shown the tiny heads and deep bodies that go with high living. The introduced fish are not expected to reproduce. It has been guessed that other rainbow strains might do so. The Bighorn is a huge trout laboratory and there has never been another like it.

At first the Bighorn was a novelty fishery to be used by anglers who had come for other streams. After a year or two there were anglers who made it their sole objective. A big river that accommodated the methods of meadow streams as well.

"The flat is very wide, water moving slowly through nearly level land." ("Bonefish Flat" on the Henry's Fork.)

EIGHTEEN

The Henry's Fork

There was a tackle shop set up at the parking lot, the operator displaying rods, lines and flies from the back of his camper. There were an even 50 cars parked in the lot and many more along the river over by Last Chance. It was peak of the season on the Henry's Fork, often said to be the best trout stream in America.

The Railroad Ranch is best known of the Henry's Fork fishing spots. That's Harriman State Park, and one of the best known parts of the park's water is what sophisticated fly rod travelers call the "Bonefish Flat." The flat is very wide, water moving slowly through nearly level land. It can be disturbing at height of the season to count 60 fishermen from one spot. Delicate dry fly fishing is seldom practiced in such neighborly surroundings. In early summer there are acres of meadow flowers, there are Canada geese overhead and sandhill cranes are nearly always within earshot some time during the day.

The Henry's Fork of the Snake River is in Idaho but near enough to Dan Bailey's shop that many of the store's customers are on their way to or from it, and the Baileys have fished it regularly. Not only does it have delicate fishing with small flies but it is noted for very large trout on a stretch of river that is a sort of magnified meadow stream. But not all of the Henry's Fork is gentle.

Briefly, the Fork begins with Henry's Lake, a famous fishing spot in itself, and many anglers make it their sole objective, casting from all sorts of craft, even from belly boats. A cluster of boats may indicate the site of an underwater spring. There are many of them. Most of the lake fly fishing is done with deep-going nymphs or streamers. It is extremely fertile water, as is the stream below it.

Immediately below the lake are several miles of meadow river that receives little pressure and has a reputation as difficult water. Then, after a marshy stretch, is Big Spring, providing a major part of the river's flow. Below that the river goes through considerable private land and down to Island Park Reservoir. Downstream from the reservoir is the Box Canyon, almost as famous locally as the Railroad Ranch.

The canyon is paved with enormous boulders, thundering water, trout and a variety of insects. Drift boats make it a little awkwardly at times when the occupants are trying to fish more water than they have time for. Waders, who get into the canyon by climbing down farther than they really want to, have backcast trouble and wading trouble but they also catch a great many good trout. They fall in frequently. There are three roaring miles of canyon.

The Henry's Fork has most of the insects of the region. Perhaps the giant stone fly nymphs and their relatives produce most of the biggest fish, but at the Railroad Ranch there is the intriguing situation of great expanses of water, dozens of skilled fishermen and big trout taking very small flies.

In June and July (the Harriman Park regularly opens in June) the most talked-of fly on the Fork is the Green Drake (*Drunella grandis*). I often stand hip-deep in the ranch water and listen to nearby anglers discussing the big drake while they hook fish on tiny things. And sometimes when a few of the great drakes, about Number 10, drift regally past the trout ignore them and take twenty-twos.

It is true that the Henry's Fork has a great many expert fishermen and that some anglers simply do not care for so much company, but while grumbling at the crowded parking spaces and the rows of casters, a logical visitor must confess that he usually has plenty of room for his actual casting. The truth is that the Henry's Fork, especially the Railroad Ranch area, has become an "in" place, partly because of the many angling celebrities who visit it every year. It is a wonderful place for name droppers and Latin speakers, and a wonderful place to catch very large trout on very small flies. There might even be a Green Drake hatch.

"Briefly, the Fork begins with Henry's Lake, a famous fishing spot in itself, and many anglers make it their sole objective, fishing from all sorts of craft, even from belly boats."

"There's some fine fishing there but for a rollicking chain of pockets joined by white water some of us have found it a bit tricky." (Gardner River.)

NINETEEN

Some Park Waters

There are fine rivers in Yellowstone Park that haven't the fame of the Fire Hole, Madison and Yellowstone. They're simply smaller and host fewer fishermen. Sometimes, but not always, the fish are smaller.

Some of them are so easily reached from a highway that serious fishermen fear they can't possibly be worthwhile. The best fishing is supposed to be a little farther back and presence of gradeschoolers overseen by their parents does not bring visions of big fish rising to fine tackle.

The Gardner River that joins the Yellowstone at the northern edge of the park near Gardiner (note that the names are spelled differently) looks easy to fish. There's some fine fishing there but for a rollicking chain of pockets joined by white water some of us have found it a bit tricky. Fish in such slanting places are supposed to be wild-eyed and grabbing for anything resembling food they can catch. Sometimes the Gardner fish hide from me.

I've caught fish on the Gardner all right but I certainly don't approach it with over-confidence. There was the time a TV producer wanted a trout fishing show and drafted my wife to appear as the star performer. In scouting the area he'd decided the Gardner was not only one of the most picturesque streams of the area but one of the easiest to catch fish from. He'd watched some fellows he considered mediocre fishermen using Woolly Worms in one of the slower pools and catching some beautiful fish. The drill, he said, was for Debie to stand in the pool, which was set in some of the best of the park's scenery, and catch a few fish for the cameraman.

Debie tried valiantly and as I recall she caught two very small trout. She also fell in, microphone and all. I wore half a mile of the

Gardner slick, as a friend of mine puts it, without catching any fish at all. This bit of drama has never made the screen as far as I know.

It isn't an isolated incident. Even during the salmon fly hatch, the Gardner River can be unfriendly to boastful fishermen. I spent most of an afternoon stumbling along the Gardner just above the northern park entrance while the gigantic stoneflies drifted down it like canoes out of control. I never saw a fish take one and I never saw one take my imitations. So I changed to smaller flies and they didn't take those either. I changed to nymphs and Woolly Worms and the only trout I saw was one I scared while wading.

But the Gardner is a fine river. Some of the biggest fish taken from it are burly browns that work into it from the Yellowstone during spawning season, sometimes charging steep water like migrating salmon. True masters of the Gardner have included the late Merton Parks, who ran a fly shop in Gardiner, a place now handled by his son Richard and his widow, Ellen. Merton was a long-time friend of Dan Bailey and one of those anglers who pulled up stakes elsewhere to make their homes in Montana trout country. As a Yellowstone River and Park guide, he was an addict of dry flies and slow to go to the big streamers, even in fall.

There is a good story about the Gardner and Ray Hurley. Hurley, who has guided for many years on the Yellowstone and on other rivers of the area, was another pilgrim who came to Yellowstone country for trout. It seems Ray was in the Parks Fly Shop in Gardiner many years ago when a visiting fisherman came in to complain bitterly that Parks flies had failed to catch fish for him on the Gardner river. The implication was that neither the flies nor the river was satisfactory. Hurley took mild umbrage at this heresy and said he could catch a legal limit of five good trout in a short time on the Gardner while using a $5 bamboo rod without a reel, using a Parks fly and nine feet of tapered leader. This turned into a wager and Hurley did the bit with a dry fly in half an hour with the visiting fisherman watching, then collected $20 from him (current price of a float trip). The visitor had become a believer.

He didn't need a reel, Hurley said, because when one of the fish proved more than he could handle otherwise he threw the rod into the water and followed it downstream. Of course Hurley has spent a great deal of time along the Gardner — but it is a testimony to fishing skill anyway.

The Gardner begins as high-altitude creeks fed by snow water. In some of the upper part the Park Service has designated a family fishing section where youngsters can use worms if they like. The fish do not run large near the river's sky-scratching beginnings.

Merton Parks, shown here on a grayling trip about 1960, was one of those who migrated to Yellowstone country. He set up a fly shop in Gardiner. He was a top angling authority.

It's down near Gardiner that most of the bigger fish are taken and that is a special place for nature lovers for a herd of antelope can usually be found in the neighborhood. The cliffs above the Gardner are favorite places for mountain sheep during the fall and it is possible to see trophy rams at times. As fall comes on outdoor photographers from around the world bring their long lenses to the Gardner country for the rutting mule deer bucks, the sheep, the antelope and the elk that are at home about Mammoth.

When Merton Parks first showed us the upper Gibbon we found it to be one of those brook trout rivulets where the main difficulty was in getting a fly to the water without hanging up or falling in. We'd been on an unsuccessful grayling expedition and Parks offered the Gibbon as a consolation prize.

Some time later I learned the lower Gibbon was a fine, although often difficult, stream for bigger fish. While I cast without result, seeing no rises on the flat runs of Gibbon Meadows, my wife engaged a good fish before an audience of tourists. She was not reticent about her method and said she had been "bubble fishing." This doesn't mean she used a spinning rod and float — simply that she was casting dry flies to little bubbles along the shoreline.

Successful bubble fishing requires a confidence I lack. To Debie, a shoreline bubble always represents a large trout. To me it can represent a submerged muskrat or even a gaseous discharge from decayed vegetation or a microscopic geyser. Anyway, I promptly began to bubble fish myself, and while Debie was catching other trout I carefully cast to bubbles apparently made by something else.

The Gibbon and Firehole make up the Madison. Elk Park and Gibbon Meadows flats give way to faster water and to Gibbon Falls, after which there is canyon water with some productive deep pools, and considerable stretches that don't even look like good trout water. But the Gibbon is a fine stream, less known only because it is overshadowed by the world-famous ones.

The Lewis River is a season-long trout stream but it is best known for the big browns that move into it each fall from Shoshone Lake and Lewis Lake. The river makes up in Shoshone and there's a world-famous stretch in the "channels" between it and Lewis Lake, sometimes a bit crowded if the reports are good in late fall.

Lewis Lake, small though it is, can be dangerous when sudden mountain storms bring high winds to cold water. It's crossed by many boaters headed up toward Shoshone. This is high-altitude fishing, just south of the Continental Divide, and it's almost 8,000 feet where the river leaves Shoshone. Just above Lewis Lake I was firmly told to take the bow when Ray Hurley and I

came downstream in a canoe to meet powerboating friends. It was getting dark and snowing pretty hard and, even in the bow, I was too busy to be too offended by Hurley's orders. I'd never been in a canoe with him before but his confident insistence upon the stern indicated he must have been experienced.

The big browns seem to run downstream from Lake Shoshone more than upstream from Lewis Lake, and in some parts of the river the fish are big enough to seem out of place in what is little more than a creek at low water. The downstream run, if that's what it is, goes against brown trout nature but is accepted by students of the area.

The Lamar River, best known for the unwelcome mud that it spills into the Yellowstone, is a good stream that picks up Soda Butte Creek and famous Slough Creek before joining the big river through a canyon. The part of the Lamar that makes the best fishing is somewhat below the mud gathering section and it's generally good for large dry flies.

From the air there's no question where the mud comes from for much of the upper Lamar runs through nearly bare and eroding mountains, which may have resulted, at least partly, from overgrazing, and the question of too many elk comes up as it does so often in Yellowstone Park ecology. To attempt seeding of the unstable bluffs would be against Park Service policy — and might not work anyway.

Some of the cutthroat performances in the Lamar and in Soda Butte are a bit startling. There have been times when good ones are caught there while holding in the steeply slanted torrents at the heads of pools. At such times they will take dry flies in the split instants that they can be made to float naturally. All of this is somewhat at odds with the usual opinions of cutthroat preferences for less violent currents. At such times the waists of the pools don't seem to produce much.

The campgrounds may be full and casters may stand shoulder-to-shoulder at Buffalo Ford on the Yellowstone, but the park has its secret spots, coveted by fishermen who choose special times or are willing to travel far from the parking lots.

"The campgrounds may be full and casters, may stand shoulder - to - shoulder at Buffalo Ford on the Yellowstone, but the park has its secret spots —"

"Work upstream with a Number 16 Dry Fly of almost any pattern and cutthroats or rainbows and occasional browns will squirt out from undercut banks and sheltering roots."
    (Shields River)

TWENTY

The Shields River

Almost everything has happened to the Shields River. It begins in the Crazy Mountains north and east of Wilsall and 40 miles of it ranges from mountain brook to slow valley stream that often looks better than it really is.

The Shields enters the Yellowstone east of Highway 89, most of it running through private property. Heavy irrigation withdrawals and silty return water have made it a problem stream. Still, in fall there are some big brown trout that work up it in search of spawning gravel and fishermen with access to the lower part have caught some fine fish. It isn't a drift river.

Many years ago when fisheries biologists stocked it I stood with Dan Bailey and saw them weigh some really big trout — but there weren't very many and very few small ones. It was several miles above the entry to the Yellowstone and although we stood well back as spectators, Dan would start involuntarily and work his hands sympathetically each time a worker lifted a big fish to the scales. Not that they weren't doing it right, but Dan obviously feared a fish might be dropped or otherwise mishandled.

The river has almost 40 tributaries with names, most of them brushy little trickles, and evidently all of them have fish — brook trout, cutthroats and often rainbows and browns. Hardly anyone bothers to fish a 2-foot creek with the Yellowstone a short drive away, but lovers of little pools like Jack Ward will insert a rod tip and short line daintily and pluck trout (often bigger than you'd expect) from miniature runs.

"If you'll stir a little mud upstream they'll get ready to feed," Jack says. "Then put a fly on top of the muddy streak and here they come!"

In fall, Jack is likely to shoot a sage grouse or some sharptail grouse and then pull an ever-present rod from his truck to finish off the day. Observers of a man sneaking up on two feet of water are likely to think he can't wade and cast, but that's not so in Jack's case. He just likes the little creeks.

Dan Bailey used to slip along the Shields where it was feeling its way out of the Crazies and catch brook trout, although somewhat handicapped by his current Labrador, which kept presenting him with sticks it wanted thrown. I reported wonderingly that I had found trout at a culvert where the water was three feet across but immediately tapered down to 10 inches once it left the road.

"In this country, if it doesn't go dry it has trout," Dan said, repeating his standard answer when questioned about creeks. Nothing seemed to satisfy him more than that answer.

There has been controversy along the Shields, and when sportsmen disagreed with ranchers on water management there have been closures. It's an individual thing with ranchers. For many years we used to fish near the ranger station on the upper Shields not far from "Target Rock" and near the "Commissary." Target Rock, looking like a shattered mountainside, will outlast all of us but the Commissary has long been reduced to scrap lumber and rubble. Dan and Helen used to camp there and those fish are worthwhile. It's hipboot water. Work upstream with a Number 16 dry fly of almost any pattern and cutthroats or rainbows and occasional browns will squirt out from undercut banks and sheltering roots. The problem is in aiming the fly across 20 feet of clear water after fitting a backcast between willows and conifers. Occasionally a ruffed grouse roars off.

The size of such a stream ruins perspective and I once announced to Dan that I had lost a 3-pound brown trout where a maze of roots shaded the deep side of a little pool, farther up than you'd expect a 3-pound brown. The fish came out after a grasshopper fly, took it with a splash and went back under the bank. I was over-enthusiastic and broke him off with a leader that should have been sufficient for steelhead. A week later I stalked my 3-pounder again.

Again there was the boiling rush, the gold-flashing turn and dash for the roots but I was proud of my controlled response that turned him and finally steered him downstream to the pool's tail. He weighed only two pounds though. A fish looks big in small surroundings.

The Shields isn't famous.

"A fish looks big in small surroundings. The Shields isn't famous."

John Bailey fishing Battle Creek as a teenager.

TWENTY ONE

Another Bailey

"Young" John Bailey, now in his thirties, answers the fishermen's letters now. He also takes their innumerable phone calls and uses a desk next to the one Dan occupied in his later years. The policy of answering inquiries has not changed although it is somewhat simplified by a Bailey map combined with stream information.

Harry Murray, the Virginia angler-writer, has the letters he received from Dan before he began his regular Montana trips. They start with general answers to Murray's inquiries and end where Dan tells him what motel reservations he has made for him.

Not all clients can accept a younger man behind the counter. One of them had misplaced his Bailey letter, received earlier at his distant home, and evidently could not believe John Bailey had written it. He quoted John's letter back to him in part and insisted that John understand what John had written weeks before. There is a sort of mystique in such things and John leaves it as it is.

The Bailey letters through the years have been international in coverage, not simply in answering questions from abroad but in giving angling information about distant waters. The Baileys couldn't fish everywhere themselves so they have compiled as much of an international file as they can from all sources.

Ask John Bailey how he learned to fish (he has a passion for it and rushes to far corners of the world with more tackle than he can possibly test) and he says:

"Look, from the first I was surrounded by world famous fishermen. Father never pushed me at all but I heard nothing else when I was quite small I kept trying to catch a trout on a fly. I didn't make it for years, I guess, and he tried to interest me in bait fishing. That didn't work because by that time I was sure there was something wrong with that."

John tried a few desultory casts with spinning gear and decided that wasn't the way a Bailey would do it either. Skimpy records indicate that he was a true pest at the store. At that time the Bailey home was on the ranch so when Johnny got out of grade school at 3:30 he would go to the store to wait for Dan. There was no telling when Dan would go home in the evening and the intervening hours regularly developed into juvenile riots. Dan had always been able to mentally shut out anything he didn't want to be bothered with so Johnny's depredations were suffered mainly by the other personnel.

John's graduation present upon finishing the eighth grade was a kit for an Orvis Battenkill bamboo flyrod and he went to work fishing in earnest. Casting distance became all-important early in his career and delicacy gave way to slashing. Remember that this was the period when distance casting became so important for the big streamers and distance was a favorite subject of conversation.

But the slashing period was only a phase and by the time he was six feet tall John began to confine his distance casting to water where it was needed. Dan left him alone. They both lived fishing but if John had preferred billiards Dan wouldn't have interfered. They did go together sometimes, of course.

"One of us would go upstream and the other down," John said, an old familiar commentary on fishing with Dan.

John became a deer and antelope hunter rather early, being a pretty good rifleman. As a kid on the ranch he had been a scourge of the local gophers, using a 22 rifle. He hunted some ducks with the family Labs, but he was primarily a fisherman. He became a competent fly tier but, like Dan, he soon stopped it almost entirely. He had to be a constant critic of the shop's output, he said. In his teens he wore the heaviest fishing vest in the West and it was a temptation to ask him for strange gadgets out of curiosity. Chances were they'd be somewhere in the recesses of his vest.

When John took charge he didn't change the store policy. The bundles of Dan's correspondence don't read much differently from what John sends out and there's generally somebody around the store to answer fishing questions, even if John is off fishing himself. They'll get you a guide but the store takes no cut from the fee — something the client often doesn't know.

If you expect a flowery description of his childhood from John Bailey you'll have a hard time, but he makes it unnecessary anyhow. He says that if he were to grow up again he'd like to do it the same way.

Dan Abrams Photo

John & Dan Bailey

Dan Bailey

Dan Abrams Photo

EPILOGUE

Following Dan Bailey's death government agencies observed his own desire for a unique memorial. He had said he simply wanted people to remember him by going fishing on a trout stream, and a great many of them have. The Montana Fish and Game Commission produced a "Dan Bailey Day" proclamation, the same in substance as that issued by Ted Schwinden, Montana governor.

The governor's version states:

WHEREAS, the Montana Fish and Game Commission with sorrow and regret, observes the death of Dan Bailey of Livingston, Montana; and

WHEREAS, Dan's remarkable life includes many significant contributions to the preservation of trout waters, the conservation of trout and the art of angling; and

WHEREAS, the accomplishments of Dan Bailey were of such magnitude that the people of Montana can be assured for generations to come that Montana anglers will have a riffle for their flies, a trout for their efforts and flowing rivers for their souls; and

WHEREAS, the special relationship between Dan Bailey and the Yellowstone River ordains that his spirit will forever dwell in its waters, and that the river will run free as long as anglers share his love and respect for the river.

Now, Therefore I, Ted Schwinden, Governor of the State of Montana, do hereby proclaim August 14, 1982 as Dan Bailey Fishing Day in the State of Montana and urge all Montanans on that day to observe the contributions of Dan Bailey that are now recorded and remembered through sparkling riffles, still pools and wild trout.

Ted Schwinden, Governor of Montana

Attest
Jim Waltermire, Secretary of State

"In his teens he wore the heaviest fishing vest in the West and it was a temptation to ask him for strange gadgets out of curiosity."
(John Bailey fishing a high mountain lake in his teens.)

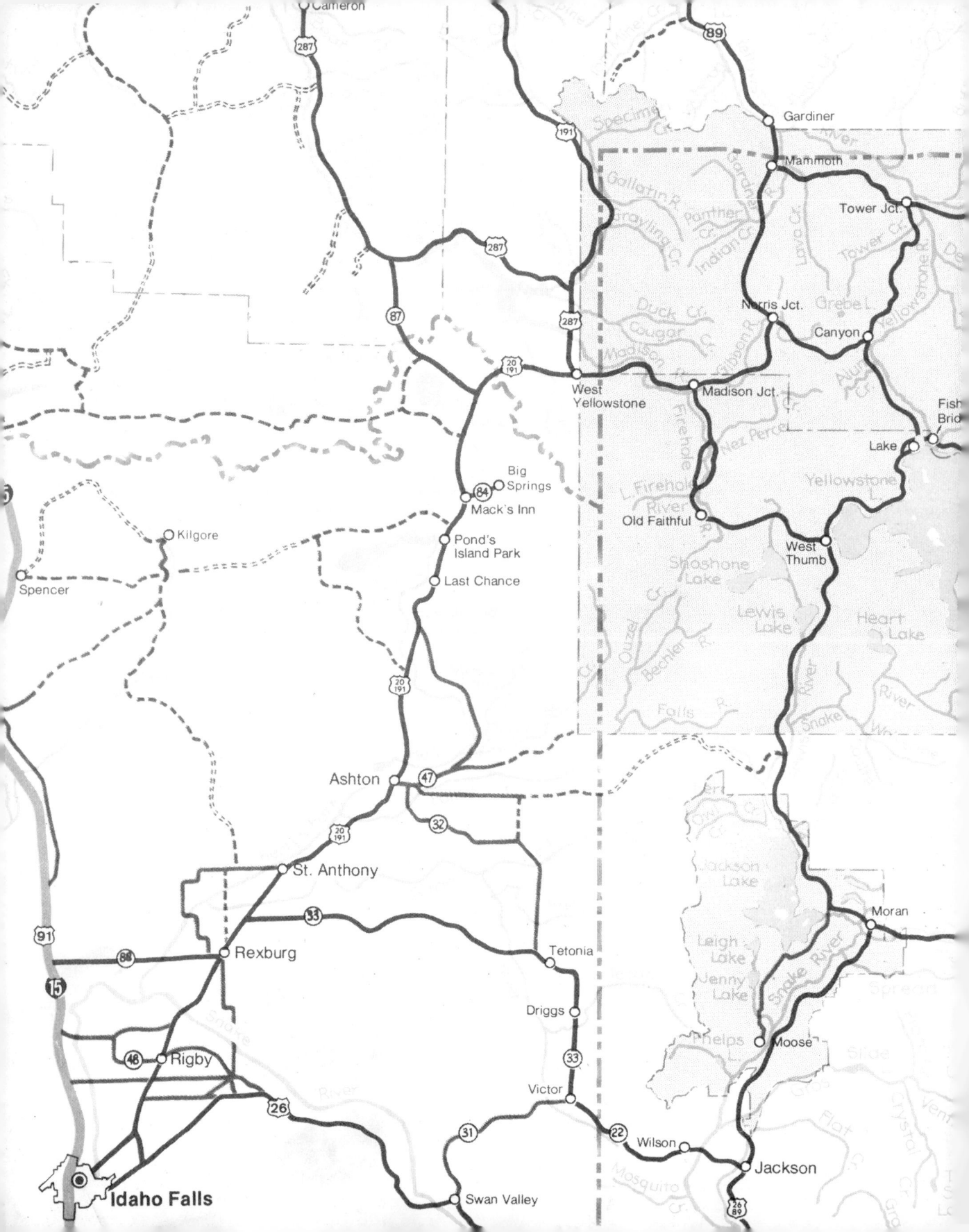